THE
LINCHPIN
WRITER

CRAFTING YOUR NOVEL'S KEY MOMENTS

JOHN MATTHEW FOX

2022, BOOKFOX PUBLISHING

"The Linchpin Writer: Crafting your Novel's Key Moments"

By John Matthew Fox

1. Reference / Writing, Research and Publishing Guides / Writing

FIRST EDITION

ISBN: 978-1-7378474-0-3

Cover design: Alan Dino Hebel of The Book Designers

Edited by Michael McConnell

Published by Bookfox Press

www.thejohnfox.com

Printed in the United States of America

CONTENTS

1

WHEN YOU BECAME A WRITER

Remember the last book you read. Now think of the book's timeline and identify where you received pleasure from it. What did you like about the beginning? Why did you keep reading? Where did you laugh? Where did you gasp? Where did you feel wonder or amazement? At what point did you stay up late, reading furiously, hungrily, because you wanted to find out what happened?

If you mapped out where you felt strongly about that book, drawing a seismograph line that spiked at maximum interest and quivered low at minimal interest, I'd wager those spikes correspond to places I'll discuss in this book. The same linchpin moments exist in nearly every book, the same critical parts that make a successful story.

What is a linchpin? If you're not mechanically inclined, you can be forgiven for not knowing. A linchpin is simply a cylindrical piece of metal inserted at the end of an axle to keep the wheel on. In days of yore, during a fair or festival, young hoodlums used to prank farmers by removing the linchpin from a wagon wheel, so that when the farmers started to roll away, their wheel fell off. This was hilarious for the pranksters, but less so for the farmers.

Over time, the word *linchpin* grew beyond that definition and expanded into the metaphorical: today, a linchpin is a person or thing that holds a complex object or enterprise together. Linchpins hold together businesses or families or governments. Or, dare I say—books.

So for the writer, linchpin moments are where the reader decides whether to abandon the book or keep reading (the beginning, the end of a chapter). These are the moments when you have a climax (surprise, main climax, emotional climax). These are the moments that lodge in the reader's brain, which they'll recall five years down the road (the ending, the death, the sex scene). If you flub up these pivotal moments, there is no amount of literary resuscitation that can bring your book back to life.

What does it look like to get these moments right? Well, there's no sense in being dogmatic about it. Every book has its own internal set of runes, rules, and powers. When I give advice, it's always contingent on whether it works *for your book*. And that's why I spend a good chunk of this book offering examples of how other writers have handled these linchpin moments: maybe the first four examples won't be right for your scene, but the fifth ignites your brain. It's my job to give you a wide range of options, across a span of styles and genres, and they can midwife you through the story.

In the end, you want to get these critical moments right because you aren't pursuing words on a page, you're pursuing how good writing makes you feel:

- The confidence of knowing this book is your best work.
- The carbonated joy when a reader tells you how much they loved your writing.
- The pride of helping your readers forget about this world as they step into yours.

Remember, writing a book is one of the most empowering things you can do in life. It's something you will never regret. Writing a book earns you a lifelong membership in a coveted and exclusive club, the Hall of Authors. This privilege can't be revoked. There is no such thing as being excommunicated or banned. But there's always that next book to write, and the firm conviction that this time, it will be even better.

I didn't pluck these linchpin moments out of a hat. These are the moments I've blogged about at Bookfox (https://thejohnfox.com) since 2006, and which more than fifteen million authors like you have used to improve their books. This is the material I've taught in my online courses for writers, which you can find on my website.

Susan Doherty used these ideas to earn a contract with Random House to publish her memoir, *The Ghost Garden*, a book that won the Mavis Gallant Prize. Bellamy Westbay used these ideas to publish her Infinity Series, Book 2 of which earned a starred review from Kirkus, which also named it one of the best books of the year. And Evelyn Bookless used these ideas to land a contract with a major publisher for her children's book *Captain Green and the Plastic Scene*, which won the Northern Lights Book Award for Best Nature/Environment Children's Book.

I have identified these linchpin moments by working with hundreds of authors as they've struggled with key sections. Then I created online resources to help them improve. (If you look at the end of each chapter, I list Bookfox posts that expand on these topics.) These are also the pivotal moments that I've worked on in my own fiction. Though I've stumbled through many valleys of rejection, by putting into practice the techniques outlined in this book, I managed to win some prestigious fiction contests and earn a contract with a wonderful publisher.

But it's not just about relying upon my expertise. Inside this book you'll get access to hundreds of the most masterful and famous writers in the world—authors like Margaret Atwood, Ann Patchett, Cormac McCarthy, George R.R. Martin, Marilynne Robinson, and Raymond Chandler and I'll draw on excerpts from their books to show you how they pull off their magic tricks. We could all use some lessons from sage storytellers (and in the process of writing this book, I gleaned plenty of wisdom as well!).

Now, if you haven't yet written the key moments of your book, wonderful—I'm going to show you mistakes to avoid and give you writing challenges. And if you have already written these moments, perfect—I'll guide you through the process of revision so you can improve those sections of your story.

By the end of this book, you'll know how to draw from techniques used by stand-up comedians and painters, explore the emotional cattle prods of soap operas, avoid the Devil Horns of descriptions, and be inspired by a fourteen-year-old writer in India. You'll also learn how paddleboarding in bioluminescent waters can help you create a sense of wonder, how a writing retreat in an Oregon cabin off the grid can help you find your ending, and how to kill a character without your readers hating you.

If I concentrated solely on the craft of writing in this book, though, I'd be shortchanging you. Just as you have linchpin moments in your book, you also have linchpin moments in your writing life. To make the magic happen on the page, you have to live a certain type of life. You have to pay attention to your writing life, and you have to deliberately take steps that put you in the path of epiphanies.

For instance, a few years ago I went to a writing conference. The most valuable part of that conference was not in the panels and not in the marquee speaker and not hobnobbing with editors and publishers. It was sitting in a trendy, upscale bar on high stools and talking with two accomplished writers. They both had successful careers and a few books out, and they were the type of writer I wanted to be in five years.

At that bar, they talked about all the major books released that year, and they had already read all of them. When one mentioned the number of books he'd read the previous year, it was exactly double the amount that I'd read—and I'm a voracious reader. The other one said he'd avoided going to the conference floor until lunchtime, because he'd spent the first six hours of the day writing. I was too ashamed to admit that I had not written at all during the conference.

It was a linchpin moment in my writing life, one that I have never forgotten. I came away realizing that the people who were making it as authors, the people who were getting the awards and the readers and the big advances from prestigious publishing houses, were simply working harder than I was. They were not more intelligent, but they were more diligent. They read more words, they wrote more words, they penned more blurbs, they reviewed more books, they attended more retreats.

Now, I could have read a thousand books about the writing life and never gotten that type of bracing lesson, a lesson that felt like getting dunked in a tank of ice water while an NFL coach yelled a pep talk. It was clear now that the major issue with my writing life was not writing technique, but simply the limited hours I was devoting to my projects. And if I could put in more hours and work more consistently, then my writing life would unspool as theirs had, with the publications and the awards and the devoted readers.

What's been your most formative experience of your writing life? As you go through this book and read about mine, I want you to make a list of your own. You should write it down in a journal: what happened and where, and what you learned from it. Ultimately, my goal is for you to not only be inspired by the critical moments of my writing life, but to come up with ways to manufacture those for yourself.

These experiences don't just happen in a vacuum. They happen because you insert yourself in the direct path of the writing life.

You go to a conference.

You attend a writing retreat.

You book a literary pilgrimage.

You enlist with a writing coach.

You take an online class.

You join an online writing community.

You order ten books about how to write a novel (oh, and actually read them!).

You start a writing workshop.

You launch a reading series.

You go to a reading at an independent bookstore and meet a friend.

If you put yourself in the pathway of the writing life, it will wallop you with inspiration that helps get you to the next stage. If you finish this book and haven't resolved to *make a writing life*, to take concrete steps of one, two, and three to fraternize with other writers and dive headlong into the world of writing, then this book will have failed to fulfill its purpose.

Now, there is one linchpin writing experience that we should talk about right now. It's the perfect one to start this book, and it's one that has already happened for you. I know, because it's happened to all of us. It's an event that every writer shares, in one form or another, and we should be thinking about it all the time. Because the way we think about this formational event ends up shaping who we are as writers.

What's the moment you became a writer?

No other moment in your writing life will be as important as this one. It's your writing birthday. But the story you tell yourself about yourself is a defining story. It determines how you act and think as a writer. If you pick the wrong defining story, it will steer you in wayward directions, and unfortunately, I know plenty of writers who picked the wrong origin story for themselves.

Many writers choose "when I published my book" as the moment they became a writer. They think that a book works like a silver badge, certifying them as a 100 percent legit, card-carrying writer. But when I got the email from a publisher accepting my first book, and I hopped on a call to discuss details before signing that contract, I wasn't any more of a writer than I was the previous week. So that's not the story I tell myself about how I became a writer, mainly because it's dangerous for my identity to be dependent on publishing success or failure. Essentially, I am who I am without the approval of others.

I've also flirted with the idea that the first payment for my fiction was the moment I became a writer. For me, it was a fiction contest with 350 other applicants for the literary magazine *Third Coast*. When they told me that the judge Ann Beattie had selected my story as the winner, and that I'd be receiving a $1,000 check in the mail, I felt, almost for the first time, that this life was possible for me.

But there's an obvious danger with starting your writing narrative based on money. Marcel Proust ending up self-publishing *Swann's Way* because no publisher wanted to risk paying him an advance. I'm pretty sure one of the titans of literature should have considered himself a writer even before publishers had a road-to-Damascus revelation and started paying him. Your identity as a writer isn't dependent on the amount of cash people will shove in your direction.

I could also think of an encounter in school as the moment I became a writer. I was at the University of Southern California, doing a graduate degree in creative writing and taking a fiction workshop with Judith Freeman, a gentle, kind, and lovely writer, and a talented teacher to boot. The class had workshopped my short story and, as was typical, spent a few minutes saying nice things and then an hour arguing with each other about what was wrong and how to fix it.

After class, Judith asked me to accompany her to her car, and we walked down in the warm darkness. The lights of Leavey Library spilled out into the quad, and undergraduates laughed in groups on the grass. We talked about what we were reading, and she asked some questions about my current writing pursuits, and then she said something I've never forgotten:

"John," she said. "You have what it takes to be a writer." She even repeated that line, as if there were any possibility I would have forgotten it.

It was the most encouraging thing anyone had said to me. Even now, thinking about it, tears well up. Because we jump into this venture with so many doubts and fears about our own talents, about whether we can actually pull off this dream. And to have an author I respected read my work and give me a hearty nod of approval, it gave me confidence for years.

But even that—the approval of a mentor—probably shouldn't be the time I identify as the moment I became a writer, even though it was tremendously empowering. Validation from others waxes and wanes. People are fickle, and you're only as good as your last book.

I think I have to go back further to find the right time, perhaps back into childhood. There was a time, when I was ten, that my mother took me to the library and helped me check out eighteen books (that was the limit). I spent the rest of the day reading. I only took breaks to go to the bathroom and to eat. I was a maniac. By nighttime, I'd spent twelve hours reading that day, and had read eleven books.

Yes, these were middle grade books, but still. Eleven books. Eleven is still my record for books read in a day. It was that day, and days like it, when I taught myself to speed read. But more importantly, I taught myself how to effortlessly drift into the universe of words and untether my imagination from my surroundings. I no longer saw the small bedroom I shared with my two brothers or the high desert landscape of California where the wind always blew in the afternoon and the temperatures were often over 100° F. It was in that bedroom that I became a believer in books: in their power to comfort and to cajole, to entertain and to emancipate. I finished those eleven books and I said, "I want to create these."

That was my first linchpin moment. That was when I became a writer.

You might think that the moral of this lesson is that being a writer starts with reading. But that's not my point. Reading is essential, of course, but plenty of people are readers without being writers.

Actually, I would argue that being a writer starts with the desire. With the passion rising in your breast. With the belief that you can tell stories. I wanted it, I wanted it more than I wanted anything else, and in that moment I was transformed from a person who merely appreciated books to a person who would spend his life chasing after their mysteries and glories.

Now it's your turn. Find the moment when you decided to become a writer and write down that story. Keep it close to you, tape it on your forehead, and write it on the tablet of your heart, because there will be times when you want to give up. When you've been rejected for the five hundredth time, or when you can't bear to sit in the chair one minute longer and stare at that messy chapter, or your book was so unpopular that not even your friends and family bought it. And you're going to need to go back to your origin story, to whisper to yourself the reasons why you decided to do this.

If you keep that story close, it will give you the power to continue.

2

WRITING YOUR
FIRST PARAGRAPH

EVEN YEARS AGO I WAS AT A WRITING CONFERENCE IN Seattle, sharing a hotel room on the seventeenth floor with four men. Three of us hadn't published a book and were canvassing the conference for literary magazine editors who wanted our stories, schmoozing with other writers at bars, and going to panels hoping to find that nugget of wisdom that could catapult us into the glorified strata of published writers. The fourth man had just released his second book, and it was all over the conference floor. His publisher celebrated it. Distributors flaunted it. Interviewers flocked to him. Panels feted him. He was, in short, the talk of the town.

It was about 5:30 in the evening when the three of us congregated back into the hotel room, trying to lick our wounds from nine hours of literary matchmaking and not feel completely and utterly overwhelmed from the flood of writing information. We were also prepping ourselves to rally and go out for yet another four or five hours of readings in dark bars. And we were looking at each other's stacks.

No, "stacks" is not a code word for a part of the human anatomy. I'm talking about book stacks. As you do at conferences like this, we had all scored dozens upon dozens of books. Poetry, narrative nonfiction, prize-winning short story collections, books on the craft of writing from authors we wanted to be like, small literary novels from one-person publishers, mid-list writers' newest novels whose work we loved, and experimental books (which we might not totally understand, but owning them made us look smart).

Alongside all the books you wanted to buy, you also have relationship buys. There were the friendship buys—you know someone who publishes a book, therefore you have a moral responsibility to buy. Otherwise, that friendship will die—not because they refuse to be friends with you, but because you're too ashamed to hang out with them because you're afraid they will ask about their book and you'll have to reveal you haven't read it. You also have professor buys. If you studied with someone, and they release a book, you have to buy it to stay on good terms. And there are sympathy buys from strangers. You see a lonely author at a book signing and take pity. Or you get into a conversation with a micro-publisher, and after ten minutes, you're in their debt, so you pick up two books.

Anyhow, we had taken our book hauls back and set them up like totem poles around the room. Fifteen, twenty, sometimes twenty-five books stacked up high. If someone didn't know better, they might have thought we were inventing a new religion, devoting ourselves to the worship of the literary gods. After we set them up, we eyeballed each other's stacks, affirming each other's choices and informing each other about fascinating books.

About this time the fourth man sauntered in and perused everyone's stack. He said nothing as he cycled through them, but we all watched him. I think all of us were both curious and in awe, because he had everything that we wanted. The adulation, the press, the awards, the critical respect, the big magazines hiring him to write profiles, the potential for a big advance on his next book, and he was even in talks with film studios to write screenplays.

I should add that this man was the best read person I'd ever met. He'd read everything. Not only the books you'd heard of but also all the books you hadn't heard of. You could play a game where you just named a book, any book, and he would tell you what he thought of it, and name three other books like it. Even though I'd read seventy books a year for the previous two decades, I felt borderline illiterate around him.

So the fourth man finished looking at our stacks, and turned like he had a grand pronouncement, and we all shut up because he was about to speak. He lifted a finger and pointed to me. "He's got the best stack," he said. We all laughed, because it did sound a little funny, like he was making a double entendre. He didn't justify his award. Just let it sit. Not that it was a competition, but I did feel obscurely proud that the best read person I knew approved of my selections.

As we kept preparing to go out on the town, one of our crew, Kris, started talking about his time in the military. He'd spent time in Bosnia and was telling war stories. About how freezing it was, especially on the top of tanks, and how there were landmines everywhere, and how so many of his stupid mates did quasi-illegal things. He said he was struggling to find a form for all these stories, though, struggling to shape them into something. He didn't know where to start. He had a thousand good stories but couldn't get them on the page.

The fourth man listened carefully to everything Kris was saying, listened without passing judgment or offering advice. About fifteen minutes into these stories, the man grabbed paper and a pen and scribbled furiously. I'm not sure the others noticed what he was doing, because they were all getting ready and listening to Kris, but I noticed. Was this what successful authors did? Randomly get inspiration and then stop everything to write it down? Was he starting his next book, right here in this hotel room, right during a conversation? Maybe I should imitate him and start writing too.

The man gave the piece of paper to Kris, who immediately stopped regaling us with his war stories.

"What's this?" Kris asked.

"It's what you said. It's your words."

Kris read it out loud. It was three sentences he had just said. But when Kris spoke it out loud, it stopped being throwaway chitchat and became something else. It was transformed into something greater, like it had undergone some kind of literary alchemy. I don't know whether it was the act of being written and then read out loud, or whether Kris read it in a different way because he was hearing it

15

properly for the first time, but these lines were new and fresh and powerful.

"That's the beginning of your book," the man said. "That's your first paragraph."

Kris began to curse. Not the angry kind of cursing, but the happy kind. Like someone crying because they're so happy. I won't go into the great variety, repetitions, and innovations of his cursing, but I'm sure that you can imagine his great skill at it—after all, he had been in the military, where basic training certifies every cadet in an arsenal of swear words.

Kris was clutching that piece of paper like a letter from a long-lost father. He read it out loud again. The fourth man nodded gravely, confirming what he'd already said. And all of us in the room knew it—this was the first paragraph of his book, without question.

Later that night at a bar, when the fourth man was somewhere else, probably receiving well-deserved accolades, and we had consumed a great deal of alcohol, Kris kept telling us: "I had no idea I was so eloquent." He repeated this line many times, apparently still in shock.

And throughout the weekend, he kept talking about that little encounter in the hotel room. I even saw him once pull the paper from his wallet and look at it again, like it was a wizard's spell he could repeat out loud and his book would simply materialize on the shelf. He was still amazed, still in disbelief. He wasn't even amazed at the fourth man's ability—that was the funny part—but amazed by himself.

What the fourth man revealed to him was his inner greatness, the writer that was always within him, the skill that he always had. He only needed someone to pull back the curtain so he could witness his true self.

16

Because of that encounter five years ago, I have devoted a good deal of time to studying the first paragraphs of books. The way they sound, the way they feel, the way they contain the multitudes of everything to come. The first paragraph of a book is quite possibly not only the most important impression a reader will get of your book, it's also the gateway for you to figure out where to start telling your story. And if you can identify the right place to start, you're far ahead of the curve. So because of its importance, it's the first linchpin moment we're digging into.

Now, to write this chapter, I went through my bookshelves and read the first paragraph of over a thousand books. This actually takes less time than you would think, and I would highly encourage you to do it with your own bookshelf. After all, most books have three paragraphs per page, so if you read a 333-page novel, you have read about 1,000 paragraphs. I mean, if you really want to become an expert at something (and first paragraphs are an *excellent* thing to excel at), then why not study a wheelbarrow's worth of the best examples?

I wanted to do several things:

- Find similarities between books. Did a number of books employ a similar strategy for the first paragraph?
- See whether there are any ways you *shouldn't* start a book.
- Learn powerful strategies for book openings.

I don't like studying first sentences of books—a sentence really doesn't give the reader enough information or the writer enough room. And besides, you've probably seen a thousand articles about famous first lines, and they all quote the same twenty, and you think, *Yeah, yeah, I know I'm not Fitzgerald or Hemingway, and this doesn't help me write my book.*

But a paragraph! Oh, a paragraph will give you enough direction to write your book, and your reader enough of a first impression to know whether they are excited to read more.

So to learn how to pull off the linchpin moment of a first paragraph, we're going to dive into the four critical components of first paragraphs:

1. Characterization
2. Energy/tone
3. Mystery
4. Emotional bedrock

If you've got those four, there is a near bulletproof chance you have a splendid first paragraph, one that will make your readers yearn for more.

Remember Jonathan Safran Foer? He burst onto the scene as a twenty-three-year-old wunderkind, publishing his first book to breathless praise and a lucrative advance. But what stuck with me was the way he talked about how he found his first paragraph. He was describing his process for writing *Extremely Loud and Incredibly Close*, his second novel, and every day before he started writing, he'd read everything he had written up to that point. As he progressed further and further into the novel, this became more difficult. Sometimes he spent over an hour or two or three reading and editing previous writing before he got to the point where he wrote new material.

And he discovered that when he read the beginning of his book, the prose didn't pop. He didn't find the energy until he got to this paragraph, ten pages in:

> What about a teakettle? What if the spout opened and closed when the steam came out, so it would become a mouth, and it could whistle pretty melodies, or do Shakespeare, or just crack up with me? I could invent a teakettle that reads in Dad's voice, so I could fall asleep, or maybe a set of kettles that sings the chorus of "Yellow Submarine," which is a song by the Beatles, who I love, because entomology is one of my raisons d'être, which is a French expression that I know. Another good thing is that I could train my anus to talk when I farted. If I wanted to be extremely hilarious, I'd train it to say, "Wasn't me!" every time I made an incredibly bad fart. And if I ever made an incredibly bad fart in the Hall of Mirrors, which is in Versailles, which is outside of Paris, which is in France, obviously, my anus would say, *"Ce n'étais pas moi!"*

So what did Foer do? He deleted the first ten pages of his manuscript. These first ten pages ended up being like Kris's war stories. They were all just flotsam and jetsam, and they prepared Foer to write the actual first paragraph of his book, but they weren't the first paragraph itself. Foer's actual first paragraph was pretty deep into the book, but he was ruthless with his writing and killed his precious early words.

What does a first paragraph like this do well? First of all, it reveals the essential human relationship at the heart of the book. Oskar misses his father, who died on 9/11 in the Twin Towers, which is why Oskar wants to invent a teakettle that reads in his father's voice. If you haven't read the book, you don't realize that connection, but Foer is already preparing you emotionally for the heartsickness this boy harbors for his dead father. This is the emotional bedrock of the book.

Also, the paragraph sets the tone and energy for this book. This paragraph zings! It's got all the high-wire tension of an electrical line, just sizzling and crackling with voltage. Try reading it out loud. It fairly begs to be read quickly and after nine cups of coffee (which might be how Foer wrote it!).

Pay attention to the punctuation. The abundance of question marks fuels the energy—the first two sentences are questions, which accelerate the reader toward the answer. And there are also two exclamation marks toward the end. What's more, when Foer does calm down enough to end a sentence with a mundane period, that sentence is more winding than an Alpine road.

Lastly, the paragraph accomplishes a tremendous amount of characterization. We can tell this is a precocious child. Precocious because he's cracking jokes in French and musing about sentient teakettles, and a child because he's making fart jokes. So we have a wonderful mix of high and low culture, which is a fair approximation of Oskar's personality. Just on the basis of this paragraph alone, I could talk to a lineup of kids and pick Oskar out.

In a very different vein, let's look at Anne Enright's opening to *The Gathering*:

I would like to write down what happened in my grandmother's house the summer I was eight or nine, but I am not sure if it really did happen. I need to bear witness to an uncertain event. I feel it roaring inside me—this thing that may not have taken place. I don't even know what name to put on it. I think you might call it a crime of the flesh, but the flesh is long fallen away and I am not sure what hurt may linger in the bones.

Now, many writers start their books with a mystery. But Enright starts with two mysteries!

First, the mystery of what happened in her grandmother's house long ago, and, second, the mystery about whether it did or did not happen. The narrator seems confused. In fact, she states her uncertainty twice, just to make sure the reader gets it.

Also, right from the beginning, Enright starts to give away the mystery. Enright calls this event a "crime of the flesh," which both withholds information (we don't know *exactly* what happened), but also gives us good guesses about its sexual nature. Beginning writers often believe that creating mystery means withholding 90 percent of the information and giving the reader 10 percent; while the opposite is true: you should give away 90 percent and only withhold 10 percent.

Don't underestimate the amount of characterization happening in this first paragraph. This is an exceptionally *careful* narrator. She's worried about the hurt in the bones that this story might cause others. She wants to write it down, but hasn't actually done so out of worry. She believes this event has happened, but also worries that it didn't. This is not an impulsive character but an exceptionally thoughtful, slow-to-act character who moves methodically and prudently.

For a third example, let's put Raymond Chandler under a microscope by checking out the first paragraph of *The Big Sleep*:

> It was about eleven o'clock in the morning, mid October, with the sun not shining and a look of hard wet rain in the clearness of the foothills. I was wearing my powder-blue suit, with dark blue shirt, tie and display handker-chief, black brogues, black wool socks with dark blue clocks on them. I was neat, clean, shaved and sober, and I didn't care who knew it. I was everything the well-dressed private detective ought to be. I was calling on four mil-lion dollars.

What's the most important word in this paragraph? The word that does more to convey this narrator's personality than anything else? I would argue it's "sober." As if being sober at eleven o'clock in the morning is an accomplishment.

Also, because he describes his clothing in such great detail, we know he's proud to be well dressed. But why is he proud? Because just like the "sober" line, he's excited that he's not in rags or naked. He has a low bar for success.

In the hands of a lesser writer, the book would go into Philip Marlowe's backstory to establish a point in time when he was in rags and drunk. But Chandler wisely starts the story at a point right when he's put together, and his amaze-ment and pride at being halfway presentable communicates

Marlowe's typical status. This is compression at its finest—always look for ways to accomplish more in a shorter space.

Now if I would buttonhole this first paragraph into a category, it would be "Description." On Bookfox and in my online courses, I usually tell writers to avoid descriptive openings, especially when they're describing the natural environment. But this description succeeds for two reasons. First, it's the description of a person, not the weather or a place. Second, and more importantly, the last sentence opens up the main action of the book: "I was calling on four million dollars."

He's making a house call for a rich client. This is the action of the first chapter, and it's going to start the mystery of the book. Essentially, a good description paragraph that opens a book will always use the last sentence to launch the reader into the action. A good rule of thumb is look squint eyed at any paragraph that is 100 percent description. Use the last sentence as a bridge to get away from mere description and tease the reader with impending action.

Think about it: the last sentence of your first paragraph is the springboard from which you launch into the rest of your book. It's the very first break in the book, and thus the first chance readers have to stop reading. Don't let them.

What's the emotional bedrock of this paragraph? Well, there are three levels of conflict that every book needs:

- Conflict with others
- Conflict with the world (a big-picture issue like poverty or injustice)
- Conflict with oneself

With Marlowe, his conflict with others is the cases he's trying to solve, the conflict with the world is his quest for justice, and his conflict with himself is overcoming his self-destructive alcoholism. The reader sympathizes with a hero who isn't perfect. We like flawed protagonists. So right from this first paragraph, our emotions tilt toward this guy.

Thankfully, the strategies for your first paragraph are uniform across all genres. Yes, Chandler's writing a crime novel, but no matter what you're writing, you can learn from him. If you look at any well-written romance, mystery, literary, YA, sci-fi, fantasy, crime, thriller, historical, or horror novel, you can mine those first paragraphs to find techniques for your own books, even if you're writing in a vastly different genre.

Learn from everything. Yes, *everything*. I've found that even genres looked down upon, like erotica or fan fiction, can teach a serious writer about pleasuring the reader and fulfilling reader expectations. Don't be snobby—be a vacuum.

There aren't many epiphanies you get as a writer. They are far fewer and rarer than we'd hope for. But standing in that Seattle hotel room, witnessing what the fourth man did for Kris? That was a moment of grace, a small kindness none of us will forget, least of all Kris.

What that man did was teach Kris to see. He taught him to see himself. To view himself as a fount of stories that will never run dry, and to believe in the stories he had to tell.

But he also taught him to separate. To separate the sentences that flop from those that prop up the narrative, and to chisel those sentences from the bedrock of chitchat and set them on the pedestal of the page.

Most importantly, he taught him where to start. If you know where to start, if you have the linchpin of a good first paragraph, the rest of your story will gently unfold before you.

I hope this book does for you what that man did for Kris.

WRITING CHALLENGES

1.   Tape yourself talking about your book. Record it on your phone, and just spitball. It works better if you're talking to an actual person, so they can ask you questions. Talk as long as you can, telling someone about the story. Then later, play the recording back and listen to yourself. Is there a particular line or paragraph that captures the heart and imagination? That lights the fuse of your story? You only need a few lines. Find your best few sentences, carve them out of that recording, and use them as the beginning of your story.

2.   Go to your bookshelf and pull off at least twenty books in your genre. Read their first paragraphs and make a list of what they're doing well, such as starting with mystery, action, energy, characterization, description, or something else. Tally up the most common strategies.

3.   Rewrite the first paragraph of your book, and make sure to use all four techniques listed above: characterization, energy/tone, mystery, and emotional bedrock.

Further Reading: Google "20 First Paragraphs Bookfox," and you can find more examples of first paragraphs, as well as analysis of what they do well.

Further Reading: Google "25 Ways Not to Start a Novel Bookfox," and you can see common mistakes when starting a novel.

3

FIRST CHARACTER DESCRIPTION

STILL REMEMBER THE FIRST TIME I EVER SAW THE WOMAN WHO would become my wife. We had just gotten out of church in Santa Monica, California, and she was talking to another man, a man I instantly felt jealousy toward. She talked with her hands and was extremely animated, as if she'd drunk an extra cup of coffee that morning. She was laughing at what he'd said and seemed like the type of person who laughed often in life. She wore a 1950s-style, simple blue dress with a fleur-de-lis pattern that narrowed at the waist and flared out to end below her knees, a dress that made her seem to come from a different era, or perhaps she didn't care about being in lockstep with the age. She was the most beautiful woman I'd ever seen.

The first time we see someone can be so memorable. Those first impressions can seed the ground for what will happen in the future. In my case, that first impression gave way to a date at Whole Foods, and then to a greasy spoon burger joint in Santa Monica, and now, fourteen years later, we have a house and seven chickens and a labradoodle and twin eight-year-old boys. And it all started with one glance.

Think about the first time you saw someone, someone who ended up playing a special role in your life. What did you first notice? Was it an element of their personality, as shown through their actions or their clothing? Was it an element of jewelry—a nose stud, hoop earrings, a clutch of bracelets? Was it their body—their size and shape, whether small or muscular? Was it the way they moved? Or was it something beyond those physical descriptors, something about their energy or their aura?

If you can tap into those memories, you'll have a reservoir to draw from when you start writing character descriptions. Borrow those real-life inspirations, add a dash of imagination, and voila! A fictional character description.

Now, I don't mean to be a Debbie Downer, but before we get into specific examples of first character descriptions, I have to point out some hackneyed ways to describe someone. You can probably guess what these are, if you think back to the last book you read or try to write a description on the fly.

I call the two most prominent clichés the Devil Horns of descriptions: hair and eyes.

Seriously, whenever I read a character description that focuses on hair and eyes, I groan a little and think less of that writer. And it's surprising, when you start noticing, just how many descriptions focus on hair and eyes.

A few examples:

- Michael Moorcock, *Elric of Melnibone*: "The long hair which flows below his shoulders is milk-white. From the tapering, beautiful head stare two slanting eyes, crimson and moody . . ."
- Iris Johansen, *The Face of Deception*: "Kinky tousled curls, only a minimum of makeup, large brown eyes behind round wire-rimmed glasses."
- A. S. Byatt, *Possession*: "He was a compact, clearcut man, with precise features, a lot of very soft black hair, and thoughtful dark brown eyes."

Once you learn about the Devil Horns, you can't unlearn it. I've condemned you to be critical of every book you read in the future, because so many books resort to this cliché! But the sooner you start thinking *Hmmm, maybe there's more to a person than their hair or eye color*, the sooner we can toss aside the trivial and dig down deep to the heart of a character's description.

Now, let's not throw stones without looking at ourselves in the mirror. Scan through your own writing for first descriptions. Are you guilty of Devil Horn descriptions? I'd wager $99 that you probably included a description of hair and eyes, at least in some of your writing. If you didn't, then kudos—you are a rare breed of writer, and I congratulate you for your originality.

Now, admitting the problems with Devil Horn descriptions doesn't mean you swear an oath to never describe hair or eyes again. It just means you realize your first impulse often swerves toward those two elements, and you have to fight for better ways to describe your character.

Sometimes (rarely) a person's eyes really are the most striking thing about them. For instance, in Frank Herbert's

Dune, eating a drug called spice turns your eyes a striking bright blue, so it would be necessary to say: "Her eyes were Fremen blue, staring out of a soft, round face."

Or you can add a metaphor to the eyes, like how J. K. Rowling describes Hagrid in *Harry Potter and the Sorcerer's Stone*: "A giant of a man was standing in the doorway. His face was almost completely hidden by a long, shaggy mane of hair and a wild, tangled beard, but you could make out his eyes, glinting like black beetles under all the hair."

A description like that is accessible. It's highly readable, and it conveys the message in a brief space. If you're writing a certain type of book, it will do. In this chapter, though, I'm going to push you to be critical of easy descriptions and to focus on writing descriptions with depth.

Other than overdependence on hair and eyes, there's a second mistake some writers make, and I call it the Kafka Trend. This is the modern tendency toward avoiding describing characters. Instead of getting into the nitty-gritty of character descriptions, the author gives a vague, impressionistic overview. Actions and thoughts are primary, sensory details and descriptions are skipped. This is an experimental technique, and it's difficult to pull off (though if you insist on being a trailblazer, I wish you good luck).

In general, the Kafka Trend is a problem. That's because we live in an age of cinema, where visual stimuli are the lingua franca of the day, and we have been conditioned, both by genetics and by our era, to want to *see* our main characters. We need to get a sense of their bodies and how they would look walking down a street. And by avoiding all types of character description, you're really hamstringing your ability to create a flesh-and-jowl person.

Some writers toying with the Kafka Trend are just being cheeky and flipping the finger at the establishment, like Jonathan Safran Foer in *Everything Is Illuminated*, who describes his main character, also named Jonathan Safran Foer, as "He did not look like anything special at all." Or sometimes the writer is telling us that the character is an everyman, like Philippe Claudel in *The Investigation*: "He was a small, slightly round fellow with thinning hair, and nothing about him, neither his clothes nor his expression, was remarkable. Anyone obliged to describe him—as part of a novel, for example, or in a criminal proceeding or judiciary testimony—would surely have found it difficult to give a detailed portrait of the man."

But enough about what we *shouldn't* do. Let's talk about how you *should* write character descriptions, which are truly a linchpin moment because they give readers their first impression of your characters. Here are four practical pieces of advice.

First, if there is a single tip that I would give you to write good character descriptions, it's this: overwrite.

Most of the time when bad character descriptions happen, it's because you trotted out the very first things that came to mind. An excellent technique is to write for five minutes trying to describe one of your characters. If you want to be brave, write ten things about them. Do it before you read the next paragraph.

Finished? Good. Now, you're going to have to kill your darlings by throwing them all away. Draw a big X over the whole paragraph or shrink the whole paragraph to five point type. Now, start again. Start fresh. Try to come up with a description of your character that you didn't think about before. What you've done is burned through all the easy answers and now you're going to excavate down to the good stuff.

I'd recommend a description that gives the reader a glimpse into the essence of a person. Take this example by Marilynne Robinson in *Housekeeping*:

> . . . in the last years she continued to settle and began to shrink. Her mouth bowed forward and her brow sloped back, and her skull shone pink and speckled within a mere haze of hair, which hovered about her head like the remembered shape of an altered thing. She looked as if the nimbus of humanity were fading away and she were turning monkey. Tendrils grew from her eyebrows and coarse white hairs sprouted on her lip and chin. When she put on an old dress the bosom hung empty and the hem swept the floor. Old hats fell down over her eyes. Sometimes she put her hand over her mouth and laughed, her eyes closed and her shoulder shaking.

When I read a character description like this, I gain a deep and abiding sense of the person. I imagine my grandmother and the shape of her body as it aged. I think about my own aging body and what lies before me. I see this character not just in a moment, but the evolution as she changed, almost as if I had the privilege of knowing her through time. This is a character description that has been poured over and emerged from the depths of long meditation.

Now, I'd like to point out something you may not have noticed: this description includes both hair and eyes. Before you string me up for hypocrisy and toss this book aside, I'd like to mention that hair and eyes are only a part of the description, not the bulk of it, and that the hair is referenced only in terms of hair loss, and eyes are mentioned not in terms of color or liveliness, but that she closes them when she laughs (they are part of a gesture, not a standalone body part). Also, I'd argue that a foundational principle of my teaching and writing process is that rules exist to be broken (yes, even the rules that I give in this book).

Yet see how much ground Robinson covers in such a short space. The beginning focuses on her head: her brow, her mouth, her skull, her skin, her hair, her eyebrows, her lip/chin. And then we witness her body through the vision of an old dress, and we observe a gesture of hers—her body language when she laughs.

Act like Marilynne Robinson and drill down to unusual descriptions, ones that strike to the heart of your character. With phrases like the "nimbus of humanity fading away," I won't soon forget the vision of this woman.

Second piece of advice: pair obvious physical descriptions with meaning. For instance, once you observe something about a character's weight or the way they shake hands, you need to explain what those elements mean, what significance they carry.

Look at this example by Dennis Lehane in *A Drink Before the War*:

> Sterling Mulkern was a florid, beefy man, the kind who carried weight like a weapon, not a liability. He had a shock of stiff white hair you could

land a DC-10 on and a handshake that stopped just short of inducing paralysis.

Wowser! Love that clipped writing that lays out not only Mulkern's characteristics, but gives them heft and bulk. Yes, he's a large man, but plenty of guys have extra weight around their shoulders and torsos. But then Lehane adds: "the kind who carried weight like a weapon, not a liability." Now as readers, we re-envision this man. He's not just some pudgy schlump, a guy who sits in the office too long and eats too much steak on the weekends. He's the type of man who intimidates with his very size. The type of man who if he feints at you, you shy away.

Now, yes, Lehane does mention hair. But to be fair, this is very memorable hair. It's a white flattop so large and even that you could land a military plane on it. The flair of the plane metaphor spices up what otherwise would be a nondescript description.

And lastly, the handshake. A lesser writer might say: "a firm handshake." Oh, but that's quite dull. Lehane makes the better decision to use the trope of hyperbole, and to talk about the handshake's power in terms of paralysis. I already feel my knuckles cracking under the pressure.

Now, consider how much of this character description traffics in violence. His very body is a weapon, his hair is a landing strip for a military plane, and his handshake can damn near kill you. In just two very brief sentences, Lehane has convinced you that this man harbors violence and has lived a life filled with violence. But he doesn't ever say the word *violence*. Sometimes the most powerful way to describe someone is to avoid using the single word that you want the reader to think about. What is most powerful is what's left out.

A third technique: contrast the physical description with the impression of the viewer. Contrast is an excellent technique because it's a micro-surprise—you expect one thing, after reading the description, but the truth ends up being something else. It's like hiding a jack-in-the-box inside your character description.

For this example, I'm swinging back to the classics, to Robert Louis Stevenson's good old Dr. Jekyll and Mr. Hyde:

> Mr. Utterson, the lawyer, was a man of rugged countenance, that was never lightened by a smile; cold, scanty and embarrassed in discourse; backward in sentiment; lean, long, dusty, dreary, and yet somehow lovable.

When I read a description about someone who never smiles, who struggles to show any type of warmth, and who appears dusty and boring, the last way I would describe them would be "lovable." But that's why this description works! The truth is that people are living, walking contradictions. A person's physical appearance, demeanor, and even actions sometimes contradict how they come off to people.

In *The Feast of the Goat*, Mario Vargas Llosa describes the dictator of the Dominican Republic, Rafael Trujillo, as incontinent and impotent. In private, his body is failing him. And yet publicly, he's feared by all and showered with superlatives: "the Chief, the Generalissimo, the Benefactor, the Father of the New Nation, His Excellency Dr. Rafael Leonidas Trujillo Molina." His bulletproof persona undermined by Llosa's rendition of his decrepit body.

Or take a lesson from Tolkien's hobbits, whose physical size is small—usually shorter than three feet—but whose resilience dwarfs all other characters in *The Lord of the Rings*. Ultimately, look for places in your writing where reality can contradict the physical descriptions. It automatically makes your description so much richer and much more fascinating.

Fourth technique: use the full power of your point of view to write character descriptions. If you're writing from the omniscient POV, most writers fail to take full advantage. They write a description with the type of information available to any shmuck on the street. You have to remember: YOU HAVE THE POWER! (imagine this in Arnold Schwarzenegger's voice).

With omniscient, you have to go whole hog. You can talk about how the character used to look, or how they will look in the future. You can make judgments about their psychology—perhaps how the character uses a specific type of clothing to hide what they consider to be fat thighs (even if they aren't overweight in the slightest).

With first person POV, the biggest advantage is that the narrator can be wrong. For instance, consider a protagonist who describes someone as appearing meek and gentle, but in the ensuing scene, she ends up having a shocking fierceness.

And a first person self-description is a generous target for the writer, with a bulls-eye so big even a freshly minted newbie will hit it. Look at the way Humbert Humbert describes himself in Vladimir Nabokov's *Lolita*: "I was . . . an exceptionally handsome male; slow-moving, tall, with soft dark hair and a gloomy but all the more seductive cast of demeanor." Uh, well, I think the reader would beg to disagree? Considering you're a pedophile diddling your twelve-year-old stepdaughter and have an ego so large it has its own gravitational pull?

In *The Art of Description*, Mark Doty writes, "To be better at description, we have to work at attentiveness." When you describe your character for the first time, you must devote your full and extended attention. You must spend time bouncing the character in the rock tumbler of your mind, seeking to know every rough edge and chipped face. When you pay attention, truly pay attention, you will dig much deeper than the shallow Devil Horns of hair and eyes, perhaps pushing through to a more mysterious description, like the way E. M. Forster described the poet Constantin Cavafy: "a Greek gentleman in a straw hat, standing absolutely motionless at a slight angle to the universe."

Remember that your first description isn't meant to be exhaustive (there's no way it can be!). It's meant to get the reader intrigued by this character and fuel a desire to keep reading. You can do this by giving concrete details that are unusual and also by creating mystery. Your goal is not only to show what is there, but hint at what the reader will learn about this character in the future. In other words, a good description is always a tease. It doesn't reveal everything. It plays coy. If you think of the first character description as the first puzzle piece of a mystery, you will have your reader salivating for more.

Pablo Picasso was a twenty-three-year-old artist in Paris, barely able to speak French and living in poverty, when the wealthy heiress Gertrude Stein bought numerous pieces of his artwork and commissioned him to draw a portrait of her. It was a steep challenge for Picasso. A successful portrait could catapult his career to the next level, or it could capsize his rising hopes. He decided to abandon caution and paint her according to his artistic sensibilities, influenced by cubism.

The result was widely derided for not looking like Stein at all, but Picasso said, "Everybody says that she does not look like it but that does not make any difference, she will." What Picasso was trying to capture in his description was some elemental essence of her, not just the outward appearance. He was trying to capture a truth about her, and apparently he succeeded, because Gertrude Stein said she was deeply satisfied with her portrait and said it represented her perfectly.

Your descriptions don't have to conform to what others think descriptions should be. You don't have to limit yourself to the most visible aspects of a person. You only need to capture the authenticity of a true soul, a human being that readers will love or hate. Be like Picasso, and paint your character not only as they are, but who your book will reveal them to be.

Alice Adams, a wonderful short story writer and teacher, never forgot the first time she saw a new student in one of her community writing workshops. The workshops were free, meaning anyone at all could join, and just before the class began, a lady in her seventies came tottering into the room. She had a delicate, tapered nose and a bob of white hair so fluffy it could have been shorn and used in a pillow. It wasn't just her age that made her walk slowly, though— she moved as thought the air itself was fighting her, and she was afraid. Most importantly, she clutched a gigantic manuscript against her chest. It was so thick that Alice worried the weight would injure her.

Now, Alice Adams was a very generous teacher and mentor, but at the same time, she was a bit worried that the lady would want her to read the entire manuscript, and also worried that it might be weird or badly written.

After class had finished, the lady came to the front, plopped the huge manuscript in front of Alice, and said, "I'm sorry. This is my first attempt at writing and it probably isn't any good. I probably won't come back next week, so don't waste your time." Her voice was shaking.

Alice kindly said, "Well, I'll read the first twenty-five pages, if that's all right with you."

"Well, you probably shouldn't waste your time," the lady said. "Like I said, I probably won't come back."

Alice took the manuscript home and promptly forgot about it. But gigantic manuscripts have a physical way of reminding you of their presence, so Alice found it a few days later, remembered she had to read it, and settled down with a cup of tea (and a pinch of trepidation—would she hate it?).

It turned out that it was not bad at all. In fact, it was much better than she'd anticipated. Actually, three hours later Alice was *still* reading. It was so good that Alice prayed that the lady would come back to class next week. It would truly be a tragedy if she never saw her again.

At class time, eleven of the students showed up, but the lady's seat remained empty. Alice's heart sank. Truly, a lost opportunity. She doubted she would ever see the woman again. Yet just as she was about to begin class, the lady tottered in.

Alice took the gigantic manuscript and placed it on the lady's desk. And then she knelt beside her. Alice was not in the habit of kneeling to anyone or anything, but she was in awe of this woman's talent and courage.

"Please keep writing this," she said. "And please, I beg you, keep coming back to this class."

The lady smiled, and she did keep coming back.

The lady's name was Harriet Doerr. She was seventy-three years old, writing her very first book, and that manuscript was a rough draft of *Stones for Ibarra*.

Soon her book was published to huge acclaim, was made into a movie, and won the National Book Award for First Fiction. She might have started writing fiction late in life, but when she started, she wrote a masterpiece.

And Alice Adams? She realized that first impressions of a character, whether on a page or in real life, can be misleading—and yet that only makes the resulting story more surprising.

WRITING CHALLENGES

1. Think of three people in your life, people who you can remember the first time you saw them. Write a paragraph that describes your initial impression. If possible, describe them without resorting to the Devil Horns of hair and eyes.

2. Find a paragraph in which you have written a description of someone and analyze it on the basis of what you've learned from this chapter. How would you improve it? What would you cut? What would you add? Would you try to make it shorter or longer?

3. Write a character description by focusing on a single salient feature. Maybe it's their hands. Maybe it's the way they run. Just one thing and one thing alone. And the rest of the description will home in on exactly why this particular thing is so memorable, and then draw personality conclusions from that single element.

4. Think of a single word that you want to use to describe a character. A word like *generous*, *thoughtful*, or *angry*. Now write a description of that character without using that word, or synonyms for that word, but that makes the reader think very strongly of that single word. For reference, look back at the Lehane example in the chapter, and how he makes you think of the word *violence* but never mentions it. If you have a writing partner, ask them to read your finished description and guess what your word was.

5. Write for five minutes describing a single character. Be as thorough as possible. Then throw it all away and start over, making sure not to use anything you came up with before. It'll be difficult, but you will push through and find a description that will surprise you.

Further Reading: Google "The Gigantic List of Character Descriptions on Bookfox" to find a repository of over seventy first descriptions of characters.

If you'd like to get better at character description, as well as other techniques, please consider taking my online course "Writing Techniques to Transform Your Fiction."

4

THE WEIGHT OF FIRST DIALOGUE

W HEN I WAS AT USC WORKING ON A GRADUATE DEGREE IN creative writing, I took a class with a grumpy old codger for a professor. You know the type—mostly retired and catfighting with the dean but the school strung him along with a single class so they could use his name in promotional materials. He was an old man who hadn't yet come to terms with the fact that he was old, and had tried every medical intervention to preserve a semblance of youth, but it wasn't working. He projected his neurosis with aging onto his fiction, writing stories of people who didn't age or a character who ages backward.

On top of that, he had an ego the size of a blimp. He spent oodles of time complaining how reviewers fifty years prior had not treated his first book fairly and had missed the references to classical literature, despite the fact that his book was viewed as a seminal text in the genre. In a *New York Times* article, he was exposed for anonymously writing five-star reviews on Amazon for his own books and wasn't embarrassed when confronted about it. He wanted the world to know that a great injustice had been done against him—no one recognized his true genius, and he was constantly undervalued. Ironically, he'd even written a book critiquing narcissism—but we write what we know, don't we?

After an introduction like that, I would guess you'd think that I didn't learn anything from his class and hated it. But here's the thing—we often learn from practitioners who are less-than-ideal human beings. One of my friends took a post-MFA workshop from a very famous writer at Chapman University, and the writer proceeded to ruthlessly mock and destroy both the fiction and the character of a woman in the class (and yet my friend said it had been the most educational workshop of his life).

The truth is that terrible human beings still have a great deal to teach about writing. Would I recommend learning from them, if you have a choice? Well, no. But I'm open to the message even when I dislike the messenger.

So despite my revulsion to my professor as a human being, I have to admit he was an excellent teacher. He assigned a huge spread of books for us to read, almost one a week for the semester, ranging from classical Greek myths to modern novels and, of course, his own book. There were only five students in the class—oh, the glories of small class sizes—and we spent three hours every Tuesday night taking these books apart piece by piece. It was clear that the professor loved these books and knew them intimately, word by word. He was good—great even—at dissecting a book, and he taught us how to do the same.

I still remember the first question he asked us about every book: *What is the main character's first line of dialogue?*

To him, this was the crowbar which could pry open a whole book. The first line of dialogue revealed everything about the book, a microcosm that contained the entire book in miniature. And as we studied book after book, we found this to be true. The first line of dialogue often showed us the character's main concern. It talked in code about the rest of the book, foreshadowing what was to come. It contained multitudes. It was—you can guess where this is headed—a linchpin moment.

It was a little like discovering a secret device that all the best writers used but which most readers weren't even aware of. If you didn't know this technique, you would probably blithely read along, even on your second reading, without considering the layers the author had baked into the book. And as a writer, if you didn't know this secret technique, you might dash off some slipshod dialogue that fulfilled the needs of the plot alone, a line with surface meaning alone but with no greater resonance for the rest of the novel. The professor taught me that the first line of dialogue was precious, virgin territory that needed to be entered slowly, with great care.

Remember that the first line of dialogue is also the first chance that a reader has to encounter your character speaking, especially if your book is told in the third person. Don't waste this chance.

Let's look at some books to see how this plays out.

In Cormac McCarthy's *The Road*, we get the first line of dialogue from the father to his son a few pages in: **"I'm right here."**

Three words, only three words. It seems simple enough. It doesn't seem to have depth. But this book is about a father and a son surviving in a post-apocalyptic wasteland. For the entire book, the father is desperately trying to protect his son from cannibalistic marauders and starvation. And for most of the book, the father is coughing up blood and knows that he's going to die soon, and that he needs to do something to try to protect his son before he passes, or else his son will be tortured and eaten by the other survivors.

So the first time we hear the father speak, he's trying to comfort his son, to reassure him that he's there for him. The son wakes up in the middle of the night and calls out for his father and his father immediately speaks up. *I'm right here*. We not only get the main thrust of their relationship in this three-word line of dialogue, we also get the main tension of the book, the main mystery that we keep on reading to find out: will the father be able to get his son to a safe place before he dies? Will he be able to keep saying "I'm right here" in the future, when his son needs it the most?

Or look at *A Thousand Acres* by Jane Smiley. Here we have the protagonist and narrator Ginny talking to her husband about another man, Jess Clark, with whom she ends up having an affair.

In her first line of dialogue in the book, she says: **"Well, then, where's he been?"**

She's showing curiosity about this man who has swung back into their hometown. This curiosity foreshadows the affair she's going to have with him, an affair that ends up threatening her marriage and the future of the farm.

This line also shows that she's suspicious of Jess Clark. It turns out Jess Clark has been dodging the Vietnam draft by traveling around the world, and that world-wandering has made him into a prodigal son, the opposite of the folks that stayed on the farm and broke their backs caring for the land. So the dialogue sets up the main relationship tension between her and Clark—she's been holding down the fort while he's been gallivanting across the globe.

I particularly like this next example by Michel Houellebecq, in *The Elementary Particles*, for two reasons: One, it's very short. Two, it perfectly characterizes the speaker.

Someone asks Michel, one of the two protagonists, what he's going to do in retirement. And Michel answers soberly: **"Think."**

Yep, one word. I told you it was short! But this straw-weight dialogue throws a haymaker's worth of meaning.

The two main characters in this book are Michel and his half brother, Bruno. Bruno is a hedonist and a sex addict, seeking and failing to find sexual satisfaction. Michel is wholly different—an introverted molecular biologist working on cloning as a way to move beyond sexual procreation.

So when Michel speaks for the first time in the book and says "Think," it's meant as a one-word characterization of him. He's a thinker. All he wants to do is think. In fact, even though he's entering retirement, he's not seeking pleasure at all, but only to continue his own scientific pursuits.

And his single-word reply helps us to differentiate the two main characters in the book. Michel's thinking is completely at odds with Bruno's pleasure-seeking. If Bruno had been asked for a single word for what activity he would be seeking, he would have said "Sex."

I'll discuss a line from Marilynne Robinson next. I am proud to have met her when I was working as a freelance journalist at the *Los Angeles Times* Festival of Books; I am less proud to have called her so casually by her first name ("Marilynne!" I yelled like a giddy schoolboy) and sang her praises to her face without even presenting one of her books for an autograph. I hope this small tribute to her genius will win me her forgiveness.

When I started thinking about great first lines of dialogue, Marilynne Robinson's book *Home* was the first that sprang to mind. The opening lines of the book are actually lines of dialogue, and before I cracked open the book, I could already remember them by heart:

"Home to stay, Glory! Yes!"

This is the Reverend John Ames speaking to his thirty-eight-year-old daughter Glory, who has just moved back home.

This line of dialogue contains so much of the tension of this book. John Ames is overjoyed that his grown daughter will spend time with him, particularly because he's growing feeble and needs help. The word "stay" is particularly loaded. It puts pressure on Glory that this shouldn't be a transitional time, but that she should be here for the rest of her life.

Yet Glory is not nearly as excited as her father to be moving back home, certainly not two-exclamation-marks-in-five-words excited. She has conflicting feelings about moving back home. She'd been teaching high school English before losing her job, and she feels like she hasn't accomplished anything in life.

And let's not forget that this first dialogue directly references the title of the book, *Home,* and all of the connotations riding on those coattails. It refers to the house itself where the family grew up. And coming home is also about embracing the code of family beliefs, including the faith of her father.

Only five words, yet the book's essence is embedded in them.

Okay, I hope I've been persuasive that the first lines your main character utters are linchpin moments and should be carefully chosen, not just trotted out to fuel the plot and start the conflict.

And you should now have enough examples to confirm that this doesn't happen by accident. Authors deliberately choose their first lines of dialogue not only to have maximum impact, but also to give the reader an additional jolt of pleasure upon re-reading (it was there all along!).

Plus, even if your readers don't realize it consciously, lines of dialogue that foreshadow what's to come and build character *prepare* the reader for the unspooling of your plot. You are laying a foundation so that when you do offer the big reveal—she's sleeping with HIM?—it lands with maximum emotional impact.

What are your takeaways from this chapter?

- *Your first line of dialogue should be short.* Look at the examples above. The longest is five words. The shortest is one word. Why? Because the longer the dialogue, the less ambiguous it is. When you just have a few words, they can be interpreted in several different ways and allude to several forking branches of your story. Preserve that ambiguity. The smaller the space, the more it can contain.

- *Don't try to perfect it in the rough draft.* You'll write this first line of dialogue in revision, on your second or third pass through the book. That's because you won't have a good grasp on the essential conflict and characterization of your book the first time through. Usually, getting the subtext right and layering in meaning can't happen until after you've bear hugged the book and wrestled it under control.
- *Think about the surface meaning and the deeper one.* Obviously, the line of dialogue has to make sense in the scene itself. That's the plain meaning, on the surface. But it will fail as a first line of dialogue if that's it. It should also have a secondary meaning. It should resonate with the deeper themes and conflicts of the book.

But you might be thinking, *John, thanks a bunch, but that's only one line.* Right—so you only need to read a thousand more chapters like this and your book will be perfect!

Seriously, though, the point is that the rules for the first line of dialogue can expand to help you with *all* your dialogue.

The care and attention that I'm encouraging you to lavish upon that first line of dialogue, you need to spread to all the dialogue you write, because dialogue should always be specialized, a heightened and powerful part of your book. Basically, it deserves more of your attention (mainly because readers will pay more attention to it).

So now that you know how to write your first line of dialogue, what are the broader implications for the rest of your dialogue? I can boil it down to four essential elements:

1. *Reveal character.* What does this line tell the reader about the person speaking? What essential core of themselves is revealed? The style of speaking should reveal who they are, and what they say should reveal their inner being. Every time a character speaks, a reader should feel like they know this character better.

2. *Support the plot.* Dialogue doesn't have to do a fireman's carry with the plot on its shoulders. That's not dialogue's job. Yet dialogue often supports the plot, helping us to figure out what's going on. It helps the reader understand how the plot is affecting the characters, which is just as important as the plot itself.

3. *Hit the emotional theme.* What's going to make your readers feel the most in this book? Aim your dialogue straight at the heart of that emotion. If it's a relationship between a father and a son, or a woman and her best friend, then dialogue has to dig deeply into the friction and love between those characters. If you direct your dialogue toward the emotional heart of your book, your dialogue will never miss the mark.

4. *Escalate the tension.* What is the main conflict in your book? Figure out how dialogue can wrestle

with that conflict. All the messiness of human relationships really is best illuminated by dialogue, by arguments and innuendos back and forth between people. We often think of tension in regards to action and plot, but dialogue plays a starring role in tension creation.

Soon after that class with the professor who was a disaster of a human being but a talented teacher, I sent out my first short story to literary magazines.

I started an Excel spreadsheet to track submissions, which listed every story, where I sent it, when, and the date of the rejection or acceptance. This was a spreadsheet that grew to a few thousand rejections before I finally stopped submitting stories and turned to book-length projects. Yes, I really did submit that many pieces to that many journals. Yes, I might be a masochist. But masochists make for good writers—or at least the persistence it takes to succeed as a writer tends to attract masochists. But back then, it was a fresh sheet with only a few lines on it, unmarred by the years and years of future rejections. I had the hope and unbounding optimism of a young writer.

The story was called "The '71." It was about a 1971 Judge GTO that a son stole from his father. The story had a lot about jail, which I didn't know much about. It also contained a great deal about blue-collar poverty, which I did know about. But the heart of it was about a son struggling with the absence of his mother and the present of his father.

I sent it to sixteen literary journals that I found on Duotrope, back when Duotrope was a free service. Most of them didn't pay, but I was hoping for two free copies and prestige. I submitted to all sixteen in January and got my first ever rejection three weeks later. Six months later, eleven of the magazines had rejected me. This was back in the days of snail mail, so the postman delivered every rejection letter in pre-stamped envelopes with my handwriting on the address, so it was like I was getting rejected by myself.

I had five literary magazines still considering it. *Fiction*, *McSweeney's*, *Green Mountains Review*, *Notre Dame Review*, and *Connecticut Review*. But were they actually considering it? When a publication takes a long time, you believe they're poring over your story late at night with a roundtable of other editors, debating its merits. You think you've survived the first few winnowings and have scored a spot in the final round of consideration, where your story has to battle in the coliseum against a grizzled group of other battle-hardened stories. Of course, it might also be that the slush pile readers are slow and haven't even gotten to your story yet. There's not really any way to tell. But hope springs eternal.

By December, I'd received three more rejections, and now I was down to only two literary magazines where it was still in contention: *McSweeney's* and *Connecticut Review*. Still, I had hope. I told my writing group that these two literary magazines had been wrestling with it. After all, it had been almost a year. Surely I'd made it to the final tier. And if I'd made it that far, one of them had to accept it.

One year out, *McSweeney's* rejected me, and I had only one more chance in the world: *Connecticut Review*. Except I had lost hope. After all, it had been a full year. The manuscript had probably gotten lost in the mail. Or their rejection had gotten lost in the mail. If it actually had been delivered to them, I figured they would have rejected me like the other fifteen magazines. Maybe my story wasn't any good. I tried to revise it, but after a few small tweaks, I didn't know what else to change. I researched more literary magazines for the next round of submissions. Perhaps I needed to send it to less prestigious magazines, ones that would consider publishing an unpublished writer like me, a guy whose bio attributed his sole writing credit to his school newspaper.

And then the moment that no writer ever forgets. The letter arrived in the mail. And it wasn't enclosed in my self-addressed stamped envelope but a typed, official-looking envelope from *Connecticut Review*. It was thick. Not one of those skimpy envelopes where you can feel the other side and the ridge of the single rejection slip inside. I opened it to find a contract and a letter explaining why they liked my story, and that they wanted to publish it in the next issue.

I danced in celebration around the house with my writing mascot, a ceramic bulldog—because, like a bulldog, I was tenacious and would persevere until I won—and sang Rocky Balboa's "Eye of the Tiger." My wife joined me for a conga line of celebration. And just like that, I was a published author.

Oh, and the first line of dialogue? It was a story about a character struggling with his mother and father, and his first line of dialogue came when he couldn't believe what had happened to his mother, about the details of her death: "You mean she's gone."

Maybe it wasn't the most spectacular line of dialogue, but I had learned from my professor: it was short, it hit at the main themes of the story, and as a young writer, it was the best thing I'd written so far.

WRITING CHALLENGES

1. What is the first thing your main character says? Look it up, and then ask yourself whether it can be interpreted in multiple ways. Does it have layers of meaning? Does it foreshadow the plot? Does it showcase the character's personality? Revise based on what you learned in this chapter.

2. Take ten minutes and write a monologue in your character's voice. It should be 100 percent dialogue, with them talking about anything, arguing about anything. Make it passionate and make it accurately reflect their character. Now be prepared to throw away everything; you only want to salvage a single line from all that freewriting. Dig among the rubble of sentences and identify the most fascinating short line. Could it be tweaked and used as their first line of dialogue?

Since so many writers struggle to write authentic, believable dialogue, I made a dialogue writing course to help them (you can find it in Bookfox Academy).

5

THE MANUFACTURE OF SORROW

THERE'S A REVOLUTIONARY CLASS IN CREATIVE WRITING THAT only a tiny number of writers have heard of. It's not available online, and the writer who designed and taught it no longer offers it. For a short window it was offered to MFA students studying creative writing at Columbia University in New York City, but if you weren't one of the lucky ones to nab a chair, there's not any way to access the course now. It's revolutionary because it pioneered a whole new way of studying novels and learning how to write, a way that broke from the traditional manner of English courses that has existed for more than a century.

The teacher was Ben Marcus and the class was called "The Technologies of Heartbreak." He and his students spent a whole semester investigating how writers made readers feel sorrow. They read books like McCarthy's *Blood Meridian*, *Revolutionary Road* by Richard Yates, and *Housekeeping* by Marilynne Robinson, as well as ten other short stories and novels, scouring them for the precise moment when a reader would feel an emotion, and pinpointing the techniques the author used to create that feeling. In the syllabus for the class, Marcus asks what seems to be a simple question: "How can a sentence, a phrase, a paragraph cause us to feel things?"

It really is a mystery: How can words create an emotion?

It's important to see that this class was truly a linchpin moment in these writers' lives. For many students it reversed a lifetime of instruction, because anyone who took English courses in high school or college or grad school had been taught to read books in an utterly different way. Before this point, every English class assumed a book is a code, and taught you to crack the code. If you failed to break the code, you have failed to be a good reader. If you did crack the code, now you had access to secret information which you could spray across a paper and get rewarded with an A. This kind of reading as code-breaking is an incredibly dismissive and reductive way to treat a book, which is unfortunate because it's the only way most readers know how to approach books.

But inside Marcus's class, they treated books like experiences. They read looking for emotional experiences, paying attention to their emotions and then deducing what techniques made them feel that way. After all, you have to let yourself experience what the author wants you to experience, and only after that point should you try to figure out how to replicate that experience in your own writing.

While reading as a code means you're trying to impose meaning onto the book, reading as an experience lets the book influence you.

If you're treating books like experiences, then you know the best way to judge a book is whether it made you feel something. It's not whether you thought something, or learned something, or whether you were impressed by the writer's skill or identified with the main character. It's whether, at certain moments in the book, the series of letters and syllables on the page made an alchemic change and stirred your human heart.

After teaching the class for a number of years, Marcus wrote a piece in the *Wall Street Journal* about the three most frequent mistakes he saw in his students' writing when trying to create emotion. Writers often use these three techniques, but all three fail to create emotion in the reader:

1. *Showing a character feeling that emotion.* When you want to make the reader cry, don't show the character crying. Watching people in a book feel emotions doesn't spark that emotion in the reader. The only thing this works for is yawning. (I don't know how it works, but if you see yawning or read about yawning, suddenly you want to yawn. Are you yawning yet?)

2. *Naming the emotion.* When the writer says, "She was overjoyed," that does not make the reader feel joy. Naming the emotion doesn't spark the emotion in the reader. Not even describing that emotion in great depth will create the emotion. We know

intellectually that the character is overjoyed, but we don't feel that joy in equal measure.

3. *Showing a character in a situation without context.* Marcus gives an example of a character who has a family member die in the beginning of a book. As readers, we don't feel grief because we don't know this character or know the dead family member. Anonymous people dying doesn't make us feel grief—there must be a relationship to cause the reader to feel sorrow.

But what *does* help writers create emotions in the reader? If you've never asked yourself this question, you're not alone. I've been a writer for twenty years, and other than Ben Marcus's class, I've only seen this question raised in a smattering of articles and books. That's disappointing because if creating emotion is the main indicator of whether a book is successful, then this is the most important question we can ever ask ourselves as writers, and improving at this skill will improve your writing more than any other course of study.

To figure out how to create emotions in the reader, we're going to turn to Edwidge Danticat. Even though she wasn't on the syllabus for Marcus's class, I have a feeling she would fit right in.

In Danticat's *The Dew Breaker*, a daughter and her father are on a road trip to deliver one of the daughter's sculptures to a famous actress. The actress has pre-paid and the daughter hopes this sale will launch her career as a sculptor, and that the actress might refer her to other deep-pocketed patrons of the arts. But at a hotel on the way, the father disappears. The daughter files a missing person's report with the police. She calls her mother in desperation. Eventually, the father turns up and confesses that he took the sculpture and threw it into a lake.

How do you think the daughter would respond to this? With anger, right? She might hit her father. She might scream at him. For an artist, there is nothing worse than someone destroying your art. Imagine your despair if someone deleted every copy of your novel.

But Danticat is far too wise to allow those prototypical scenes to play out. The father and daughter are standing, looking at the lake, and the daughter (the story's narrator) speaks first:

> "Is this where the sculpture is?" I ask.
>
> "In the water," he says.
>
> "Okay," I say calmly. But I know I'm already defeated. I know the piece is already lost. The cracks have probably taken in so much water that the wood has split into several chunks and plunged to the bottom. All I can think of saying is something glib, something I'm not even sure my father will understand.
>
> "Please know this about yourself," I say. "You're a very harsh critic."

Most beginning writers would show their character's anger in an attempt to make the reader feel anger. But we don't need that! As a reader, I feel horrified and so sad and angry on her behalf, because I know as an artist what this would do to me. The *situation* is what creates the emotion in me, the action of a sad event happening in the storyline, and not the character's reaction to that event.

This is exhibit A to teach you that the character doesn't have to feel something in order for the reader to feel it. In fact, the character can feel something completely different than what you feel, and the author could well have intended that. I'll go even further—making the reader feel one thing and the character feel another thing is an excellent technique, because that friction forces the reader to grapple with the character's unusual reaction. Here, the daughter is feeling something more like resignation, while I'm feeling angry and horrified on her behalf.

After that, the book goes back in time to show when the father met the mother after seven years apart. They'd been married in Haiti, but the mother stayed in Haiti while the father took a job in New York City. And Danticat offers us a moment that we all know well, the moment when they met at the airport. The reunion makes the reader feel joy:

> Then suddenly she found herself before a door that slid open by itself, parting like a glass sea, and as she was standing there, blinking through the nearly blinding light shining down on the large number of people who had come to meet loved ones with flowers and placards and stuffed animals, the door closed again and when she moved a few steps forward it opened, and then she saw him. He charged at her and wrapped both his arms around her. And as he held her, she felt her feet leave the ground. It was when he

put her back down that she finally believed she was really somewhere else, on another soil, in another country.

Note that Danticat doesn't mention any of the emotions she wants you to feel. She doesn't name joy or happiness. All she does is describe the physical activity between this husband and wife. They run toward each other. He lifts her body from the ground. And yet the reader feels the weight of their joy because a reunion is a universal event that everyone understands, and so we project our own experiences of reunions onto this scene. And because seven years is an exceedingly long time, longer than most of us have been separated from someone we love, we feel those raised stakes, and our emotional reaction is heightened because of it.

Let's move to another emotion that Danticat explores: sorrow. In this scene, a former boyfriend, Eric, is calling Nadine:

> Whenever he called her now, which was about once a month since their breakup, she removed the microcassette from the answering machine and placed it on the altar she had erected on top of the dresser in her bedroom. It wasn't anything too elaborate. There was a framed drawing that she had made of a cocoa-brown, dewy-eyed baby that could as easily have been a boy as a girl, the plump, fleshly cheeks resembling hers and the high forehead resembling his. Next to the plain wooden frame were a dozen now dried red roses that Eric had bought her as they'd left he clinic after

the procedure. She had once read about a shrine to unborn children in Japan, where water was poured over altars of stone to honor them, so she had filled her favorite drinking glass with water and a pebble and had added that to her own shrine, along with a total of now seven microcassettes with messages from Eric, messages she had never returned.

A shrine to your aborted child is one of the most heart-wrenching things you can imagine. Every detail adds to the weight of this: the drawing of the baby, the roses as a consolation gift, the messages from the ex-boyfriend. And we're primed for this sorrow because at the beginning of the scene, we're sad about their breakup. It's like Danticat wants to give you one thing to feel sad about, and while you're caught up with it, she sucker-punches you with a scene a thousand times sadder.

Now, it's impossible to create shrines-to-aborted-babies emotions on every page of your book—honestly, it would get exhausting for the reader—but we live in a culture that demands a steady stream of dopamine hits from our entertainment. What's a writer to do? Well, you should use micro-emotions on every page.

For instance, here the mother remembers her harsh parenting style: "By offering neither each other nor their daughter any presents at Christmas, Anne and her husband had tried to encourage her to be thankful for what she already had—family, a roof over her head—rather than count on what she would, or could, receive on Christmas morning." This isn't the most devastating line, but it does make the reader ache for this child deprived of Christmas presents.

There's another micro-emotion when the father recalls what his employer said to him: "There's tons of people like you in this city. Half of them need a job." Just this single line of dialogue from his boss makes him feel disposable and worthless, and we feel pity for him.

So what has Edwidge Danticat taught us about emotion?

1. *Situations cause reader emotions.* Danticat writes to an audience with artistic sensibilities, so someone destroying a piece of artwork would likely pain them.

2. *Create contrasts between character and reader emotions.* Strive for characters with counterintuitive emotions. That builds character and lets the reader feel emotions without strong-arming them.

3. *Micro-emotions on every page are essential.* If you've left the reader feeling nothing, that means the page is on its knees, begging for a rewrite.

In September of 2001, I arrived in New York City to start a master's degree program in literary theory at New York University, and one week later the planes struck the Twin Towers. At the time I was renting a room on the twenty-first floor of an apartment building in the East Village, and when I threw open my tin-foil-covered shutters, the towers were spewing smoke from holes punched in their flanks. My camera was a disposable one, one in which you roll the black dial to advance the film, and as the first tower fell, I was both horrified and desperately scratching that black dial to the right to document the moment. After they fell, I did exactly what I promised my mother I wouldn't—I went downtown, hoping to help.

Hordes streamed by, covered in white dust like mimes. Groups huddled around cars with all doors open, blasting the radio. The bridges were packed with shuffling bodies like refugees from a war-torn country, and the air was corrosive, with a scent like burnt wires. I got as close as I could to Ground Zero, until the smoke and dust were so thick I could only dimly see the emergency lights of a police car. It was like looking into the mouth of hell. I stood there all alone—everyone else had already fled—and realized I was utterly powerless against the scope of this devastation.

That was my introduction to New York City, and I don't think I ever recovered. Fast-forward through two lonely, poverty-stricken years, living in a slum twelve stops out on the L line with a nickname of Poverty Palace, above a drug den, where someone got murdered on my street corner, and struggling to eat more than one time a day, I decided to abandon my studies in literary theory and focus on creative writing. I had stories and thought people needed to read them.

So I applied to MFA programs. Thirteen of them, to be exact. I picked dream schools and I picked safety schools located in urban centers and tiny pastoral towns. Even though I was destitute, I scraped together $1,200 for application fees and mailing costs (saving by eating less and never going out). And then I waited. I waited for the next stage of my life to unfold before me. I was finished with Barthes and Derrida; I wanted to be the next DeLillo or Pynchon.

Within a few months, twelve of the programs had rejected me. I held out hope for that thirteenth, one of my safety schools. In the end, they waitlisted me. I was first on the waiting list, so surely someone would choose another school and create space. Then came a final letter: all six writers they'd accepted had committed to the school, leaving no spot for me.

I was twenty-three years old with a mountain of student loan debt and a master's degree that left me utterly unqualified for anything. So I slunk back to my parents in the desert town of Palmdale, California, and worked the graveyard shift at a Rite-Aid warehouse. From 9 a.m. to 3 a.m. I stood in front of a giant wall filled with toothbrushes and deodorants and hair gels, and when they lit up with a number, I put that number in a bin. After a few hours, my brain went numb and my body didn't belong to me. I thought I was smart, but the MFA programs had disagreed. I thought I was smart, but I was working a minimum wage job at night in a warehouse. I thought I was smart, but I was still unpublished.

Still, I could write, right? So I wrote. Story after story. And tucked them into beige manila envelopes with self-addressed envelopes and courteous query letters and mailed them to literary magazines with high hopes. I wish I could report back from this time of my life with good news. I wish this was the part of my story that stopped being so depressing and where there was a marvelous and joyous surprise. But the truth is that the successes are often few and far between for writers, and you have to slog through a swamp of rejections to get there.

Yet I did press on. I kept submitting and kept writing because I believed that eventually I would get better. And, yes, I finally got the contest wins and the prize money and publications in prestigious literary magazines and a book published with a wonderful publisher—but only after wading through a channel of manure.

It's almost comical when writers tell me they're beaten down because they've gotten ten or twenty rejections for a book or a story or an article. If I was an unkind person, I would probably laugh. Because, honey, you haven't even started yet. You better grow a spine of steel if you want to be in this business. You better ironclad your ego and never swerve, or else you'll flop.

But then came a linchpin moment: I joined a writing group.

After going to the University of Southern California for a fully funded graduate degree in creative writing, I moved down to Orange County, where I found a group of writers with the tongue-in-cheek name of The Biscuits. They were graduates of the Chapman University MFA, all serious and talented writers. We met at our houses or local bars like The Olde Ship and drank British beer while eating fish and chips and bangers and mash and sticky toffee pudding. Once a month we'd show each other our work and offer in-depth critiques.

And we had a contest. Oh, what a contest! You got points for submitting, you got points for writing (based on word count), you got points for acceptances, and we kept track of it all in a spreadsheet and were completely serious and yet not serious at all. The winner got fun prizes like a free meal or a beer or bragging rights, and it was a healthy way to push each other to keep the writing streaks alive.

We drove to conferences together. We drove to readings. We went on writing retreats together at rented houses.

We mourned each other's losses when a beloved dog died. We celebrated as members got married, had children. We started a band together (holla to Wheel House!). We lived the writing life together, and without their fellowship and their support and their guidance, I couldn't have been a writer. So many writers think of the degrees they need to be a writer, or the epaulettes of writing awards, but all you need is a group of people who will swear they won't let you quit and promise to carry you when hardships have injured your soul.

One member bought us all literary mugs. Another one bought us all hats with the name of our writing group on it. We sang carols together at Christmas and debated the latest books and movies while in hot tubs. And then we started publishing books, and we went to signings and left nice reviews on Amazon and Goodreads and played cheerleaders. Because we were a team.

Until we weren't. Until it all felt apart.

Two members abruptly moved up to San Francisco for work. And then there was a wicked fight between the two remaining women, over a hundred things, including a relationship with a man, and there were accusations of jealousy, and of dependency, and of betrayals, and in the end, the friendship that had anchored the group suffered an irrevocable split.

I didn't realize how much I had until it was all gone. Now, every time I'm driving on the freeway at night, I think back to my late-night journeys coming back from five-hour writing meetings, and the comradery, the banter, the drinking, the book discussions. I've never really found a replacement for that group, probably because suburbia isn't a bastion for the arts. There aren't any independent bookstores or readings. People are teachers and plumbers and lawyers and therapists, but never writers. Events happen in Los Angeles, but with traffic, that's a roundtrip commute of two and a half hours. The writing life can be an awfully isolating experience, and though I'm alone now, I will always look back fondly on the many wonderful times I got to spend with that group.

I miss them. I miss them and don't know if I'll ever have a writing group like that again. We were so young and flooded with optimism, truly believing that we could make it in the writing life. I long for it every day, the sense of belonging to a team—the way we'd throw our arms around each other's shoulders and soldier on.

I leave you with this benediction: May you find a writing group full of good souls who write daily and tell you to do the same. May your to-be-read piles be stacked high with their recommendations, and may you fiercely debate the merit of newfound books. May you find friends who are writers and delight in their friendship, and may the friendship come before the writing, but also may you never forget the writing. May you travel together, conference together, retreat together, and dream together. May your manuscript critiques be made in love, and received with grace and humility. And may you find writing success, however you define success, alongside them.

WRITING CHALLENGES

1. Read a chapter of any book and write an emotion in the margin every time you feel something. Not when you're supposed to feel something, but when you do feel something. Make sure to notice even the micro-events that stir emotion. A single funny line, a single mean phrase, a description of a run-down house. Now look over your marginal notes and figure out *how* they made you feel an emotion.

2. Writing Challenge: Pick a boring and inanimate object, like a hat or a marble or an extension cord. Now in the space of a single page, make the reader feel a strong emotion about that object. Fear, sorrow, joy—any single emotion counts.

3. Here's a micro-emotion challenge: Make a reader feel sad in less than fifty words. I'll give you an example.

When my friend was a teenager, she told her mother, "I hate my nose—I want a nose job." Her mother said, "Absolutely, honey. I'll make an appointment right now." But my friend felt disappointed. She'd really wanted her mother to tell her that her nose was beautiful.

6

JOURNEY TO THE WONDER

W HEN I READ GREAT FICTION, IT WORKS ON ME LIKE A DRUG. It slips down my throat and enlarges my senses. I'm stunned, in awe, and acutely aware of a feeling of generosity pulsing off me in waves, dousing everyone around me. I have to put the book down and bask in the glory of the world for a moment, allowing myself to feel drunk with the brightness and fullness of space around me. My heart feels two sizes larger. My entire body is carbonated—rising, rising. I'm filled up with thankfulness toward language and the spells it can cast over me, and I want to direct honor and appreciation toward where it is due.

I've just tried to describe my bodily sensations when I'm reading and feel *wonder*. If it sounded abstract, that's because it is. Wonder isn't like sadness or happiness or jealousy, or any of the normal basket of emotions we feel a dozen times daily. Wonder is rare. Yet I think it's worth talking about, and worth telling writers to strive to create.

I'm aware that what will provoke wonder in readers is highly subjective. But when I stood at the base of Angel Falls in Venezuela, after traveling for a day and a half in a puddle jumper plane, then in an outboard canoe, and hiking on my own two legs, and together with eight other people stared up at the water that fell so far it was transformed into mist, no one was unmoved. The beauty of our world reliably delivers feelings of wonder. So if there's that much similarity in our human brains, there must be equally reliable ways to induce the same emotion of wonder using language and stories.

David Foster Wallace nailed why more writing instructors don't talk about wonder. He said that when you get feedback from a beta reader or editor, they tend to focus on easy, teachable things, "the sorts of simple, surface concerns that a dozen or so people can talk about coherently: straightforward mechanics of traditional fiction production like fidelity to point-of-view, consistency of tense and tone, development of character, verisimilitude of setting, etc." And yet Wallace bemoaned that it's much more difficult to talk about the things that truly determine the greatness of a story: "little things like interestingness, depth of vision, originality, political assumptions and agendas."

To that second list of Wallace's, I would add wonder. It's remarkably difficult to talk about creating wonder in your fiction. And when I create online courses and talk to writers about their writing, it's tough to talk about intangible things like wonder. So I want to seize this chance by discussing it in a book. It's too important of a reading experience to avoid.

As I've thought about times when I've experienced wonder in stories, I've realized they often occur when I'm reading about worlds or creatures that lie just outside the realm of my comprehension. Things so strange and wonderful that I can't fully grasp their beauty or enormity. I can't bear-hug it with my brain and wrestle it into neat categories and make it make sense. I can only dimly apprehend it as if in a mirror.

For instance, I kept trying to figure out what I liked so much about Jeff Vandermeer's Southern Reach trilogy, and when trying to justify it to my book club, I finally articulated it: Vandermeer made me feel wonder. He made me marvel. And in the first book of that trilogy, *Annihilation*, in which an all-female expedition pushes into a mysterious Area X where animals and humans mutate at astonishing speed, Vandermeer made me feel wonder at the climax, when the protagonist describes the Crawler for the first time. The Crawler is an entity crawling down a spiral staircase, inscribing words on the wall, and is so otherworldly I was flabbergasted:

> Did I say I had seen golden light? As soon as I turned that corner entire, it was no longer golden but blue-green, and the blue-green light was like nothing I had experienced before. It surged out, blinding and bleeding and thick and layered and absorbing. It so overwhelmed my ability to comprehend shapes within it that I forced myself to switch from sight, to focus at first on reports from other senses.

The sound that came to me now was like a crescendo of ice or ice crystals shattering to form an unearthly noise that I had mistaken earlier for buzzing, and which began to take on an intense melody and rhythm that filled my brain. Vaguely, from some far-off place, I realized that the words on the wall were being infused with sound as well, but that I had not had the capacity to hear it before. The vibration had a texture and a weight, and with it came a burning smell, as of late fall leaves or like some vast and distant engine close to overheating. The taste on my tongue was like brine set ablaze.

No words can . . . no photographs could . . .

As I adjusted to the light, the Crawler kept changing at a lightning pace, as if to mock my ability to comprehend it. It was a figure within a series of refracted panes of glass. It was a series of layers in the shape of an archway. It was a great sluglike monster ringed by satellites of even odder creatures. It was a glistening star. My eyes kept glancing off of it as if an optic nerve was not enough.

Did you notice that every one of the character's senses fail? Her eyes can't discern the colors, her ears can't hear the music properly, the smell she can only describe through metaphor, and the taste is beyond description. This creature is otherworldly. It's the most beautiful and most terrible thing the character has ever experienced, and she feels completely inadequate before it. And this interaction with the Crawler goes on for six more pages, six more pages of feeling our limitations and trying to describe the indescribable.

The closest analogy for this passage would be the Book of Ezekiel in the Old Testament, when the prophet is describing God surrounded by living creatures as wheels within wheels, and the fiery whirlwind filled with creatures with four heads and covered with eyes. Ezekiel keeps on using simile after simile, and metaphor after metaphor, because comparison is all you have when reaching beyond human comprehension.

You might know Michel Faber from his book *Under the Skin*, which was made into an odd movie featuring a terrifying and nude Scarlett Johansson. But I'd like to talk about his follow-up, *The Book of Strange New Things*, in which he tackles an equally strange universe. It's literary sci-fi about a missionary evangelizing beings on another planet. And check out how Faber describes one of these being's faces:

> Here was a face that was nothing like a face. Instead, it was a massive whitish-pink walnut kernel. Or no: even more, it resembled placenta with two fetuses—maybe three-month-old twins, hairless and blind—nestled head to head, knee to knee. Their swollen heads constituted the Oasan's clefted forehead, so to speak; their puny ribbed backs formed his cheeks, their spindly arms and webbed feet merged in a tangle of translucent flesh that might contain—in some form unrecognizable to him—a mouth, nose, eyes.

He starts the description by denying what it is: the face is not a face. And then he attempts one metaphor with the walnut, abandons it, and tries for a second metaphor with the placenta. In the next paragraph, he admits that the placenta is also a bad description, but he can't help but compare it to something that he knows. Just like the Vandermeer example, we see a character who has reached the limits of his understanding and flails beyond those boundaries. It's even stranger when, later in the book, we see the creatures give birth from their face (I'll spare you the visceral details of that quote—less wonder, more revulsion).

And then the way Faber describes the planet is equally staggering. We are on a planet that is utterly foreign to us, a world we have never seen. And the slow and deliberate way Faber treats this place makes you believe it's real, that he has been an eyewitness:

> The sky's color was elusive; the gradations were too subtle for the eye to discern. There were no clouds, although occasionally a patch of air would shimmer and become slightly blurry for a few seconds, before shivering back into transparency. . . .
>
> Up ahead, two bodies of rain were coming into view. By chance, the sun was perfectly positioned in the clear space between. The peripheries of each body of rain shimmered with subtle rainbow colors, like an inexhaustible launch of noiseless fireworks.

Faber's great skill is that he depicts a place where the world is relatable, but vastly different from ours, in such imaginative ways that you're left slack-jawed. It's not wild and crazy, it's just the normal weather of a planet we've never experienced.

I wouldn't want you thinking that wonder is only an emotion for sci-fi stories, though. Our world is perfectly strange as well. Look at the way Cormac McCarthy describes a group of men riding their horses at nighttime in *Blood Meridian*:

> That night they rode through a region electric and wild where strange shapes of soft blue fire ran over the metal of the horses' trappings and the wagonwheels rolled in hoops of fire and little shapes of pale blue light came to perch in the ears of the horses and in the beards of the men. All night sheetlightning quaked sourceless to the west beyond the midnight thunderheads, making a bluish day of the distant desert, the mountains on the sudden skyline stark and black and livid like a land of some other order out there whose true geology was not stone but fear. The thunder moved up from the southwest and lightning lit the desert all around them, blue and barren, great clanging reaches ordered out of the absolute night like some demon kingdom summoned up or changeling land that come the day would leave them neither trace nor smoke nor ruin more than any troubling dream.

That "soft blue fire" is an example of St. Elmo's fire, where the upper atmosphere gets so charged with electricity that it sinks down and creates mini-lightning glows at ground level. But McCarthy never uses the phrase "St. Elmo's fire," and the passage is better because of it. Naming the phenomenon would rub off some of the luster of the otherworldly nature of this experience.

I can see that blue fire on the horses and the men, and see the sheetlightning illuminating that barren desert, and their diminutive troop in the vastness of that landscape. This isn't another world but our world, yet it's such a rare and fantastical scene that I'm in shock every time I read it, instantly transported to that strange realm. Plus, the arch language from a bygone era, part Shakespearean and part Old King James, adds to my sense of wonder.

Now, if these excerpts didn't light up your synapses, you should remember that their power is greatly diminished in isolation. As I was reading, I was steeped in their world for hours and hours, and *then* I hit a passage that split my brain down the center, where I felt the dawning of wonder. Which makes wonder an even more rare emotion than sadness or humor—those I can both evoke in a single line, but to get to wonder, I have to hypnotize you with my words and slip you deep into a dream. Wonder takes time to build.

Okay . . . it's time for me to admit to misleading you. The whole of this chapter has been a kind of magic trick— I've used a sleight of hand both with the chapter title and the ostensible subject. Wonder is certainly a worthwhile topic, but there's also another topic in this chapter hiding in plain sight. Take a look back at all the examples I gave above. What do they all have in common? What type of writing are they? If you look closely, you'll notice they're all *description*.

But rather than starting with description on the blackboard, I think it's better to start at the end point, at the emotion that good description creates, and then work backward from there. Not to say that all good description creates the emotion of wonder, but only that when you're writing description, you want to start with the emotion and then figure out how to describe the place or object. There's no such thing as a good description that doesn't create an emotion.

What does bad description look like? Well, it's transactional. It gives the reader the information they need to progress through the scene. But that's a remarkably low bar for description. Like so many other things in writing, description is mainly useful as a way to create a mood or emotion, and not merely to appease the reader's senses.

You should use your descriptions to do one of two things: to either defamiliarize the familiar, or to familiarize the unfamiliar. In other words, if you're writing about a place that would be familiar to the reader, you're trying to make it feel strange and fresh and new to them. And if you're writing about a place that is essentially strange and foreign, you have to use metaphor and all your sensory tools to allow the reader a handhold on the identity of this place.

One summer night my friend asked me to drive to Newport with him because plankton in the water was causing bio-luminescence. My sole experience with bioluminescence was when, as a child, I'd read Jules Verne's *20,000 Leagues under the Sea*, and I'd marveled at all the passages where Captain Nemo and crew encounter the glowing water: "The *Nautilus* was floating in a phosphorescent stratum, which was becoming dazzling in this darkness." I was eager to see it in person for the first time, so at nine o'clock at night we launched our paddleboards from under a bridge at Back Bay. The water, disappointingly, didn't glow at all, but we hoped to find a place where it did.

The fog hung low and thick, so it felt like paddling through a tunnel. It was so foggy I worried about boats not seeing us. The scuttle of our boards over the water was the only sound. As we rounded a bend and got into a sub-channel filled with the hulking shadows of yachts, there it was—at the tip of our paddleboards and around the curves of our paddles, the water glowed an electric blue. Not just a muted hint of color like from a glow-in-the-dark toy, but a bold, bright, effusive blue, a blue belonging on a neon sign. It only lit up when we disturbed the water. We were laughing and in shock as we dipped our paddles. We found even darker parts of the channel, hidden from the lights of houses, and where the glow shone ever brighter.

And the fish! It took us some time to realize that the shooting stars beneath the surface, the blue zig-zagging streaks, were fish. In the blackness of the water, we could never see their bodies, we could just see their paths, illuminated in bright blue lines before fading back to black. We even startled some small schools of fish, which felt like watching every star in a galaxy suddenly swap places.

We reached the main channel around eleven o'clock. The fog was still thick. We were the only ones on the water—we hadn't seen a boat in the last half hour. We pushed forward into the darkness and the fog until all the houses disappeared from view and all we could see was the water, the fog, and the phosphorescence around our paddles. It felt like the surface of a different planet. My heart was so full of gratefulness and pleasure that I sang. A simple hymn of thanksgiving. And then we paddled back through the glow of blue waves.

I've never forgotten the wonder of that night. I don't know how I could experience something else that's so otherworldly, so magical, so bizarre. Our video footage from that night was so remarkable that a local news station broadcasted it. My friend actually paddleboarded multiple other nights, although it was never as brilliant as that first night.

I feel honored to participate in a profession that gives people the feeling I had that night. A sense of wonder isn't easily replicated and isn't easily created, but when you use the power of language to fill up your readers' hearts and brains with what they could never imagine themselves, they will thank you a thousandfold for it.

WRITING CHALLENGES

1. Describe a mundane, everyday object in a way that will make the reader marvel.
2. Describe the most unusual place you've ever visited in a way that makes the reader afraid, jealous, angry, or astonished.
3. Describe something that lies just outside the realm of human comprehension. This could be extraterrestrial, spiritual, supernatural, or surreal. Use as many metaphors as possible, but show that these metaphors have limits.
4. Identify a time when you've felt wonder when reading a book. What was the author doing? Now, choose the same subject area and attempt to imitate that author. Your words will be entirely yours, but the framework will be borrowed from that author. Write a paragraph that will give your reader a sense of wonder.

7

THE LANGUAGE OF LOVE AND DESIRE

A LINCHPIN MOMENT FOR YOUR READERS IS THE CLIMAX OF A romance. For some younger characters, this might be verbal: they say "I love you" for the first time. For other characters, it might be a long-awaited and passionate kiss. For many adults, a budding romance leads to sex. Whatever that physical affection looks like in your book, please don't botch it up.

But I've got bad news: the odds are against you. Most writers, even talented writers, start writing a physically romantic scene only to pratfall in comedic and tragic ways. Romantic scenes are often badly written screeds of the author's naked desires, gratuitous imagery, metaphors for genitalia that don't pass the sniff test, and spit-takes of twisted prose. And if you're confident that you'll be able to pull it off, please don't be: when it comes to this area of writing, your confidence is inversely proportional to your skill.

If you want to take a tour of the history of bad romantic writing, you don't have to go further than the Bad Sex Awards. Since 1993, the British publication *Literary Review* has highlighted a winner and shortlisted four titles that all featured cringe-inducing intercourse. It's the literary equivalent of a Razzie, and yet some authors are good natured enough to come take their award in person. Yes, in person—because there's a four-hundred-person party at a military club in the heart of London, where, with much fanfare, double entendres, and drinking, they raise mocking toasts to writing that shot its load far off the mark.

It's hilariously awful to read the excerpts. Kimonos with giant bulges that were "seized, kneaded, massaged, squashed and crushed." Penises that are "as soft as a coil of excrement." Wince-inducing phrases like "her moist parts to my triumphant phallus." And metaphors gone wrong, so many metaphors gone wrong, especially those involving animals such as elephants, monkeys, and boa constrictors. Please, for the love of good writing, don't use animal metaphors.

Still, when I was studying how to write good sex scenes, I grew frustrated that the Bad Sex scenes sucked up all the attention on the internet. Whenever I searched for *good* examples of sex scenes, I couldn't find any. I mean, I found the classics, like the scenes in *Lady Chatterley's Lover* and *Tropic of Cancer* that got both books banned, but nothing modern. So as a man of action I set about solving that problem, and compiled fifty sex scenes on Bookfox so other writers would have a repository to study (check it out—you know you're curious).

Now, you might be a fade-to-black writer. Meaning: you lead the reader right up to the sexual moment, and then pull out, giving them some privacy. The tale resumes with both of them staring up at the ceiling, offering post-coital quips, or when morning light greets them. And there's nothing wrong with that. In fact, depending on the genre, such as YA or fiction for a conservative or religious audience, it might be the required thing to do. Or it might just be a matter of your own preference and style of writing, your instincts leading you toward subtlety and away from the explicit.

But some stories demand stepping into the bedroom. On occasion, the characterization requires it because what needs to happen between these two characters can only happen during physical romance—exposing selfishness or showing unnecessary roughness. Sometimes it's a critical component of the plot—betrayal, role play, submission, domination, lack of protection—that leads to the next step in the narrative. And sometimes it's a matter of writing philosophy, a determination to show the totality of a character's life, and not shying away from the hidden or the unspoken experiences of being human.

The Italian writer Elena Ferrante, the most famous writer of the modern era who cloaks her identity under a pseudonym, has her character Elena go out to promote a book she's written, a book with a notable erotic encounter on a beach. Elena goes to a university, and a tall, thin, nervous girl asks her why she wrote the "risqué parts." At first Elena is embarrassed and blushes. But then she says something remarkable: "I spoke of the necessity of recounting frankly every human experience, including—I said emphatically—what seems unsayable and what we do not speak of even to ourselves."

Every part of this response is critical. First, books don't have to shy away from any human experience. If it has ever happened to a human being, it is worthy of inclusion in a book. It doesn't matter if it offends someone or breaks a taboo—the role of books is to say what seems unsayable. The things that we know in some deep part of ourselves, but what we never have verbalized. Only in this way can the book be an axe for the frozen sea inside us. Only with this type of honesty and candor will books survive the onslaught of competing media and still have a vital role to play in human development.

When I'm writing these things, I'm always trying to convince myself as much as anyone else. See, I grew up in a conservative Christian environment, going to faith-based schools from kindergarten all the way through four years of college. It was a world that separated the genders to different spheres, that encouraged a model of courtship rather than dating, and I even knew some female homeschoolers who were so prim they refused to shake a boy's hand. Wearing purity rings was popular, to remind yourself to stay pure until your wedding night. Of course there was very little sex education, and we were not allowed to read books in our English class with any type of "risqué scenes." I was so sheltered that as a junior in high school, when one of the kids at school asked whether oral sex was okay before marriage, I thought he meant talking with someone in a sexy way, and I said that sounded fine to me.

It's taken quite a lot of courage and reexamining of my own values to climb out of what others might call a repressive culture, but what I would describe more diplomatically as a culture that prizes old-school virtues of respectability and honor. I've had to struggle with the boundaries I believe in as a writer, with what I was willing to write and not write. After all, we are often our own worst enemies as writers. Self-censorship is the most common censorship. We get in our own way because we carry a lot of the burdens of cultural and familial expectations. But I started to believe that a writer always has to challenge the norms and rules of society, or else they are not fulfilling the prophetic role of a writer.

As I wrestled with how to write sexual material, I realized I was feeling a lot of shame. Shame about how all my friends would perceive me. They would think I'd left the faith because I had the audacity to write "smut." They would throw away my book in protest or, even worse, leave a bad review on Amazon. And I also doubted myself: Was I just reacting in a kneejerk way to the conservative culture of my youth? Was this just a rebellious fling? Was I going for shock value rather than asking what the story needed? But I took comfort from this quote from Karl Ove Knausgaard, the prolific Norwegian memoirist:

> But as anyone with the least knowledge of literature and writing—maybe art in general—will know, concealing what is shameful to you will never lead to anything of value. This is something I discovered later, when I was writing my first novel, when the parts that I was ashamed like a

dog to have written were the same parts that my editor always pointed out, saying, "This, this is really good!"

An unfiltered honesty—about everything in life, including sex—is essential for the writer. If you feel shame about some part of your book, whether it's memoir or fiction, that's a sign it'll connect with your audience. They will love that you stripped away pretense and told the unvarnished truth. If you can embrace those feelings of shame and push through the uncomfortable writing, those will be the parts that people email you about, thanking you for your honesty.

But enough justification of *why* we should write intimate portrayals of romance—let's move on to how writers can do it well.

The best way to start to think about good romantic writing is to figure out what it isn't. What is the opposite of good sex writing? I would argue that it's erotica. If you write erotica, I'm sorry, but what I have to say in the rest of this chapter probably won't help you. Erotica has the sole goal of arousing the reader, and everything else becomes secondary.

I'm going to suggest something counterintuitive right now, but I would actually recommend you attempt to write a short passage of erotica. Yes, I am fully aware I just told you *not* to write in this genre, but hear me out. Many writers, when they first start to write a sexualized scene, resort to bad stereotypes and sloppy descriptions, things they've absorbed from popular culture—the same things that inspire erotica. So without noticing it, writers slip into bad habits, and those will haunt their writing.

But if you *try* to write that way? And laugh at yourself while doing it? Oh, then you'll know what to avoid. You'll meet your flawed writing head-on and expose its faults. You'll see its flaws as you write it.

So bust out every cliché, every snort-inducing nickname for genitalia, every over-the-top line of dialogue, every implausible scenario, and get it all out of your system now. One of the best ways to learn how to write well is to try to write badly. So indulge your inner sensualist and have a fling with this writing challenge.

Okay, now that you've taken a stab at writing it, let's run down the main flaws of erotica, and how it helps teach us how *not* to write a sex scene. Erotica fails in four distinct ways:

1. It boils complex sexual encounters down to biological exchanges focusing on body parts and physical sensations. It depicts characters more like machines than humans.

2. The singular goal is to arouse the reader, rather than show characters on a journey or show the full range of human emotions.

3. It elevates sexuality to the end-all goal of human existence. Hedonism becomes the philosophy of life.

4. Despite some minor tension preceding the sex, in erotica the sex is always wonderful. It's a fantasy version of sexual relationships.

Janet Fitch, the author of *White Oleander*, taught me the principles of that first point. She said that in erotica, body parts are always the actors. The penis stabbed. The breast wobbled. The thigh quivered. Every human being is dissected into erogenous zones, and those disembodied body parts play with other disembodied parts until they finish with a heave. Until round two . . .

But in real sex writing, it's always the *whole person* who acts. She thought this, he felt that, she caressed him, he combed her hair. People interact with people, rather than body parts with body parts. This type of writing treats human beings like whole and complete beings rather than sex toys fused onto torsos and legs.

As for the second point, your main goal is to show the psychology and emotional development of these characters. Titillation is more of a secondary effect. Mainly because when you show the characters feeling insulted in bed, or trying to please their lover and failing, or being generous to their partner, you're going to remind the readers of their own foibles and successes in the bedroom and outside it, and connect with them on a much more intimate level than merely getting them off. They will see themselves in this character, and the character's life will speak into their life. This is a textured richness of life that can't be replicated in erotica.

For the third point, every book promotes a vision of the world. When you write a sex scene in an erotic style, it promotes a stripped-down version of hedonism. In a caveman voice: *Pleasure good. Pain bad* (unless pain leads to pleasure, you sadist). Sex is all that matters in life, and you should spend the majority of your existence seeking to get your rocks off.

When you say it out loud, it sounds like the philosophy of a horny high school boy, but it's surprising how many people stumble into this mindset. The French writer and provocateur Michel Houellebecq has actually been accused of this type of reductionist thinking about sex because he writes so many sex-obsessed male characters. Ultimately, I hope you want the purpose of your book to go beyond mere hedonism. Aim higher.

And fourth, only in erotica does sex partake entirely of the fantasy where everything goes swimmingly. I'll admit it's nice to read fantasy. But between real people, sex is often not that way, and even if it was, it would be boring to keep reading about perfect sex that does not involve you.

Okay, so if that's what good sex writing *isn't*, what *does* it look like? You're probably pent up with anticipation, so let's take a look at Lauren Groff's compact example in her novel *Arcadia*:

> Her mouth moved down, then farther. He touched the top of her head, her fragile skull under wet hair, pulled her up gently. He wanted slowness, warmth, kissing. But she wouldn't. She grasped him, though he wasn't quite ready; she wasn't either, she was dry, still cold. But she moved just slightly, sitting there above him, and after a few minutes he took the bones of her hips and pulled himself in until he'd fully stirred. She pressed down again, her body against his chest, and at last her mouth found his. He imagined the quiet street outside shining in the lights, the millions of souls warm and listening to the rain in their beds. He couldn't stop looking at the side of her face, her eyes closed, the small shell of her ear, the scar in her nostril where the stud had been, her thin

pale lower lip in her teeth. He was close but held off, until at last she whispered, Go. I can't come.

Hotdog, that is a damn fine scene. Low-grade conflict sizzling right at the beginning (and yes, like every other scene in your book, conflict is essential). He wants slowness, she doesn't. She's willing to go down on him, but against all expectations he refuses it. The typical gender roles are reversed.

This is not just an example of conflict; it's also an example of psychology. Psychology is as crucial in a sex scene as the sex; if you forget this, every sex scene you write will seem limp. Notice the character-building gestures at the end that certify them as thoughtful partners: He's close but holds off out of respect and concern for her. And she's gracious enough to prioritize him by telling him to go ahead. Here we have two characters who are being selfless in bed—an example of love and not just sex.

While in a sloppily written sex scene, everything is cock-swelling, vagina-blowing euphoric, in this scene we get a mirror of real life by encountering problems, at least three of them by my count:

- He's not hard initially; she's still dry.
- They want different things.
- In the end she can't climax.

Pay careful attention to the language, particularly what is absent: there's no formal language like *penis* or *vagina*, and no slang like *cock* or *pussy*, and certainly no silly or over-the-top euphemisms like *Mr. Stiffy* or *vajayjay*. Instead of grasping for the easiest and most typical language of "hard,"

Groff chooses softer, more roundabout language by saying that "he wasn't quite ready" and later on that he'd "fully stirred." Instead of talking about wetness, Groff writes that the character was "dry, still cold." In the last sentence, she doesn't say "climax" or "orgasm"; the character says she can't come.

Even when talking about her face, Groff doesn't use the word "cheek," which could make the reader think of buttocks, but she goes out of her way to use the unwieldly, shambling phrase "side of her face," which nimbly sidesteps any connotations. There are no sexual positions mentioned, only the position of their bodies in relation to each other. Groff doesn't even use a low-key G-rated word like "kiss," instead preferring the phrase "her mouth found his." It's rare to find a passage of writing that is incredible for all the language it *doesn't* use, but I would recommend this one for an award (a Good Sex Award!).

When Groff does talk about body parts, it's not the body parts you'd expect. The character describes a closed eye, ear, nostril, and lips. Almost as if the camera of his attention is tight against the woman's face. By talking about what your character is noticing, you can subtly inform the reader of the position of bodies without acting like a director of a play and staging bodies.

Lastly, don't miss the step-away moment in this scene. Every sentence in this paragraph stays inside this room . . . except for one. Did you notice it? "He imagined the quiet street outside shining in the lights, the millions of souls warm and listening to the rain in their beds."

Quoted out of context, it doesn't seem to belong in a sex scene. Wouldn't that misdirection deflate the erotic energy?

But it comes at a critical moment, right after they kiss for the first time. And it feels like this kiss ignites the man's imagination, and he floats away for a moment to a beautiful scene beyond them, to all the couples in their beds just listening to the rain. It's a touching and beautiful moment that accentuates all the action inside the bedroom, connects them to the world at large, and also mimics real life by showing that when we're having sex, we're not always concentrating on the sex—minds wander. Also, adding a little step-away moment helps to slow down the scene and the pacing so the readers can process this critical moment more leisurely.

Jeffrey Eugenides, in *The Virgin Suicides*, portrays a sexual escapade between two teenagers as an attack, with the girl flinging herself on the boy:

> He sat in his car, gazing at the house, watching as downstairs lights traded places with those upstairs, and then, one by one, went out. He thought about Lux getting ready for bed, and just the idea of her holding a toothbrush excited him more than the full-fledged nudity he saw in his own bedroom nearly every night. He laid his head back on the headrest and opened his mouth to ease the constriction in his chest, when suddenly the air inside the car churned. He felt himself grasped by his long lapels, pulled forward and pushed back, as a creature with a hundred mouths started sucking the marrow from his bones. She said nothing as she came on like a starved animal, and he wouldn't have known who it was if it hadn't been for the taste of her watermelon gum, which after

the first few torrid kisses he found himself chewing. She was no longer wearing pants but a flannel nightgown. Her feet, wet from the lawn, gave off a pasture smell. He felt her clammy shins, her hot knees, her bristly thighs, and then with terror he put his finger in the ravenous mouth of the animal leashed below her waist. It was as though he had never touched a girl before; he felt fur and an oily substance like otter insulation. Two beasts lived in the car, one above, snuffling and biting him, and one below, struggling to get out of its damp cage. Valiantly he did what he could to feed them, placate them, but the sense of his insufficiency grew, and after a few minutes, with only the words "Gotta get back before bed check," Lux left him, more dead than alive.

Hells bells, that's a scene. Eugenides, that maestro of the page, orchestrates such sharp contrasts between the characters' experiences. All the conflict comes through the boy's point of view:

- He feels like his marrow is being sucked out.
- He feels terror.
- He feels disorientation—he didn't even know who it was at first.
- In the end, he feels entirely insufficient to satisfy her.
- After she's left, he feels more dead than alive (he's been consumed).

And even though we don't get to see the scene through the girl's perspective, we feel her overwhelming sexual hunger and desire, mostly conveyed through comparisons to animals. Eugenides breaks the rule I mentioned at the beginning of the chapter, about avoiding animal metaphors, but he manages to pull it off here for two reasons: he compares her to an unusual animal, an otter, which doesn't run over the spike strip of cliché, and he also compares her to an imaginary animal, a creature with a hundred mouths, which uses hyperbole to dramatic effect.

Did you notice the scarcity of dialogue? The one line of dialogue at the end doesn't have anything to do with sex: "Gotta get back before bed check." There's also an element of danger in that dialogue—she knows she's breaking the rules by sneaking out of the house and has to sneak back in before she's caught.

Pay attention to the sensory details of the scene. That perfect detail of watermelon gum—I can almost taste it right now. We also have touch: clammy shins, hot knees, bristly thighs, oily fur between her legs. Eugenides includes smell as well—the pasture-like scent from her grassy feet. And the scene begins with sight, as he watches the lights move from downstairs to upstairs. Sound is underplayed, but he hears a snuffling, and then she speaks to close off the scene. Hope you were buckled up, because Eugenides just took you on a five-senses ride.

This scene even advances the plot. This daring escape for a brief sexual encounter shows how trapped the five sisters are in this religious household, and why the restrictive prison of their house might have contributed to their suicides. It builds the legend of the sisters to a mythic status. Also, this event contributes to the girl's characterization—Lux is renowned for being lustful, and this scene shows the reader that desire in action.

If you're yearning for another example, let's look at Toni Morrison's *The Bluest Eye*:

> I stretch my legs open, and he is on top of me. Too heavy to hold, and too light not to. He puts his thing in me. In me. In me. I wrap my feet around his back so he can't get away. His face is next to mine. The bedsprings sounds like them crickets used to back home. He puts his fingers in mine, and we stretches our arms outwise like Jesus on the cross. I hold on tight. My fingers and my feet hold on tight, because everything else is going, going. I know he wants me to come first. But I can't. Not until he does. Not until I feel him loving me. Just me. Sinking into me. Not until I know that my flesh is all that be on his mind. That he couldn't stop if he had to. That he would die rather than take his thing out of me. Of me. Not until he has let go of all he has, and give it to me. To me. To me.
>
> When he does, I feel a power. I be strong, I be pretty, I be young. And then I wait. He shivers and tosses his head. Now I be strong enough, pretty enough, and young enough to let him make me come. I take my fingers out of his and put my hands on his behind. My legs drop back onto the bed. I don't make no noise, because the chil'ren might hear. I begin to feel those little bits of color floating up into me—deep in me. That streak of green from the june-bug light, the purple from the berries trickling along my thighs,

Mama's lemonade yellow runs sweet in me. Then
I feel like I'm laughing between my legs, and the
laughing gets all mixed up with the colors, and
I'm afraid I'll come, and afraid I won't. But I know
I will. And I do. And it be rainbow all inside. And
it lasts and lasts and lasts. I want to thank him,
but don't know how, so I pat him like you do a
baby. He asks me if I'm all right. I say yes. He gets
off me and lies down to sleep. I want to say something, but I don't. I don't want to take my mind
offen the rainbow.

Giddy up! That right there is a fine passage. She's good.
No, she's great. Morrison's wickedly wise use of repetition
on the ends of her sentences makes us feel the bump and
grind of the sex. Repetition is one of the oldest tricks in the
books to covertly show a sexual act—think of the end of
James Joyce's *Ulysses*, with Molly Bloom repeating *yes* time
and again, mirroring her ascent into orgasm: "yes I said
yes I will Yes."

The power dynamic is marvelous. While we might think
of a woman being on bottom as an act of powerlessness,
Morrison's character Pauline views it as an act of control—
with her legs wrapped around him, he can't escape. She
wants him to come first, and when he does, she feels the
power she has over him. And even his ability to make her
come reveals her power to herself—she's confident enough
to allow him to do it.

Writers such as Michel Foucault and Camille Paglia have
argued that all sex is about power, and while that seems too
transactional to me, I'll admit that as a writer, you should

be paying attention to who has the power in your sex scene, and how they are wielding that power over the other person. Remember that power is much more complex than it initially appears: we might suspect an older man has power over a younger woman, but you have to account for the power of beauty, youth, wealth, social connections, workplace dynamics, and personalities, which can muddy up simplistic assessments.

I can't get enough of the way Morrison describes the female character's pleasure. What a clever technique of synesthesia, where sensations become colors. The little bits of color float up, and then the green june-bug, purple berries, and Mama's yellow lemonade. A rainbow represents her orgasm. And in the second paragraph, instead of focusing on the outer actions of fingers, tongues, or other body parts, Morrison goes wholly inner, focusing on a colorful way to describe this character's sensations.

Look, I hope those three scenes gave you a jolly good read (oh, and helped your writing). In the end, you just need a plan when you write a linchpin scene with physical romance. Because I want to make it easy on you, here are seven steps:

1. Know how this scene develops the characters' personalities and sense of self as well as their relationship.
2. Sketch out how this scene could possibly further the plot—does this event lead to something? (And not just pregnancy—it could be jealousy, a realization that they need to break up, or a dissatisfaction with their relationship.)

3. Realize what emotion you're trying to provoke in the reader (no, not merely arousal—consider humor, fear, astonishment).
4. Hammer some problems into the scene, even if they are small problems, so you don't end up with a cheesy scene with all roses and rainbow orgasms.
5. Nail the power dynamic between your characters.
6. Determine the language you'll use for genitalia, if you're going to refer to them at all.
7. Include risk for the characters, not just physical risk but emotional risk, or the breaking of taboos, so you have tension in the scene.

And lastly, have fun. How many people get to say that they get to imagine sex scenes for work?

WRITING CHALLENGES:

1. Write the worst erotica you can imagine, with hyperbole, crazy euphemisms, hilarious dialogue, and unbelievable psychology. Afterward, figure out what elements of erotica you want to avoid when writing real sex scenes.
2. Write a sex scene composed entirely of dialogue, with no descriptions of physical movement, but let the reader guess the basic contours of what's happening. Somewhere in the scene, sneak in this line: "Don't do that."
3. Write a sex scene without mentioning a single body part. Focus on descriptions of the rooms, the person as a whole, and the narrator's thoughts.

Further Reading: To read more examples of sex scenes, google "50 Incredibly Written Sex Scenes in Books" and you'll find my article on Bookfox.

8

THIS IS HOW YOU END A CHAPTER

I COULDN'T FIND THE ENDING. IT WAS A STORY I'D WRITTEN FOUR times from scratch, each time failing in some way. I had thirty-three separate files on my computer, with each of the four drafts containing about eight different versions. And it was still wasn't working—mainly because I couldn't find the ending.

See, endings are not something you discover at the end of your story. Like: *Bing!* The lightbulb goes on and the entire story now makes sense in retrospect. Endings are what you start with. You picture in your mind's eye the way that the chapter or story will conclude, and then you write toward that, funneling all the separate pieces together until you end at the place that ties the story together. Except I had broken that rule and hadn't started with the ending, and now I was chin-deep in the swamp of despair.

I had tried everything. I had solicited feedback from both of my writing groups. I had emailed friends from graduate school and gotten written feedback that was very, very long, so long it was frightening. I had let the piece lie fallow and come back to it after six months with a whole fresh concept. I read it out loud, multiple times, and threw it away and started over; I read books on craft, and consulted my mentors, and pulled my hair, and prayed to God almighty to give me a revelation, and read a gazillion examples that I could possibly imitate. But nothing was working.

Why did I keep going on this story? Why not just throw it into the "unpublished" folder on my computer, where it could rot and fester until some university bought the treasure trove of unpublished papers after my death? (ha ha, fat chance). I mean, at some point you have to throw in the towel and admit you've been beaten and bludgeoned beyond even what Rocky could have taken.

But I kept searching for an ending because I loved this story, and I loved this story because it had been inspired by my friends. See, one of the happiest times in my writing life was in my mid-twenties. I joined a writer's collective of a couple friends, and we rented a house, a house we called the Jack London House because Jack London frequently hosted writers and artists gatherings in San Francisco. Every week we had a gathering of writers, thinkers, scholars, and artists, when we would have soirees and readings and snacks and drinks (always drinks!).

We turned off the lights, lit fifty candles, and recited our invocation as a group—a poem called "Ode" by Arthur O'Shaughnessy. "We are the music-makers, we are the dreamer of dreams." Then we listened as people read out loud what they'd written recently—poetry, nonfiction, fiction. When they finished reading, the audience did not clap, but only snapped their fingers: a gentle pitter-patter of appreciation that was dignified, classy. And then we would talk and debate and drink and rank books and roar with laughter and argue into the wee hours of the night until everyone slouched home with ballooning dreams of the future.

The members of this house, who were like brothers to me, had watched a brief video by National Geographic about a lost world in Indonesia called the Foja Mountains, a place only accessible by helicopter and so remote that virtually no modern human had explored it. It was teeming with undiscovered wildlife and was so virgin that nobody even knew whether natives lived there. My housemates planned to fundraise to hire a film crew to fly there and make a full-length documentary. We would discover new species, perhaps even a local tribe, and explore a place as untouched as the moon. We would be feted as brave pioneers and celebrated internationally.

Unfortunately, like many ambitious plans of twenty-somethings, it fizzled out and never happened. Except a decade later in my story. Because this is the advantage of the fiction writer over the nonfiction writer: you can explore in your imagination what you can't explore in real life. As I did extensive research and wrote this story, it felt like I was fulfilling our dream, our dream to explore the unexplored, to take fantastic trips together, to be the world-changers. As the Jack London House broke up, as people moved away, got married, had kids, slid into grown-up jobs, and lost the freewheeling artistic vibe of their twenties, I'd pined for that spirit of comradery and art, as well as the unbridled optimism of my youth. If nothing else, I wanted to write this story for them, to flesh out what could have been. If I failed at this story, it would have been a second failure, not only to make the documentary, but also to redeem the high hopes that our friendships were founded upon.

And then, as I struggled with ending this story, a writing friend suggested a writing retreat. Not just any writing retreat, but one at her family cabin up in Oregon. And not even a house, but a small remote cabin exceedingly far from civilization. No cell phones—they didn't work. Not even any roads—I did say remote, didn't I? The only way to get there was by boat.

This was it, I thought. This was my moment to carve a week out of my life and figure out the ending to this story. I said yes, even though I was married and the other two writers were women, which gave my wife pause. But they were good souls, so in the end she gave her blessing and our trio of writers did a two-day road trip up to the Rogue River, where we chartered a small skiff and took a thirty-minute upriver journey to the remote cabin.

I'll never forget my first vision of that place. The water scudding against the boat bottom, the roar of the boat engine, eagles wheeling in the expanse above us, and then the river took a turn and there was a dock, and fifty feet up a hill, a tiny cabin, smaller than I had imagined, with a long front porch and a stalwart chimney, isolated by thousands of acres of wildlife and forest. It looked like paradise.

We lugged our bags up the hill, waved goodbye to the boatman, and opened the door without a key. You didn't need locks out here. It had two bedrooms, a bathroom, and a generator for electricity. This was protected national land, one of only three family cabins on the Rogue River, each built in the early 1900s and passed down through the generations. There was no way to rent these cabins and certainly no way to buy them.

After a few minutes puttering around, we started writing. Yes, right then. After two days full of driving, where all I did was think and imagine, I had so many pent up words that I had to let them out. I got four hours solid in at the desk that night, and broke off only to talk with my literary comrades just before we went to sleep.

The next morning I went running. The boat driver who dropped us off had warned us about local mountain lion sightings (and there were always bears, of course), but I still decided to run along the foot trail that led upriver in the early morning, glancing behind myself whenever I heard a suspicious crack of a twig. The danger of being mauled seemed small next to the absolute paradise of running in the wilderness, the glorious way even the birds are cheering you on. Besides, running helped me to think about my story, to consider what I had written so far, and to continue to mull over the ending.

Being on a writing retreat helps to dispel some fictions you tell yourself about yourself. For instance, normally I can write for only two or three hours, four hours max, before I peter out. It's almost like a rule I have: I quit after two hours. But on writing retreats like this, when I'm with other people who are laser-focused, and there are no phones and no emails and no pressures from work, suddenly, magically, and invigoratingly, I could write for nine hours a day.

This wasn't the only writing retreat I've been on—I've done weekends in Laguna Beach by myself in the cheapest hotel I could find in off season; I've done Palm Springs with five other writers in a house filled with more than seventy taxidermied trophies from African safaris; I've been snowed in by a blizzard and run out of firewood and had to boil water for heat during a writing retreat in Big Bear; and I've done a three-day bender outside Chicago when I played hooky from a conference. But this Oregon retreat was my favorite. Not only because it was one of the most beautiful places in the world, but because the essence of a writing retreat is being separated. Separated from your normal people, your normal life, your normal pressures. Most importantly, it's about being separated from technology. Without phones and televisions, you only have your imagination. A writing retreat strips your life down to its most basic elements: you need to eat, you need to sleep, and you need to write. Nothing else exists.

To a writer, that's paradise.

My fellow writers were knuckle-deep into their own projects. One was writing a novel about Croatia and the other had just finished a biography about one of the Disney magnates and was working on short stories. We kibitzed about each other's projects at nighttime. As far as my own writing project, I had introduced an entirely new dynamic into the story, making one of the main characters struggle with infertility, which was a personal issue for me at the time—my wife and I had been trying to get pregnant (and failing) for almost two years. And that character's brother in the story had a problem with *fertility*—he kept getting girls pregnant and then aborting the kid. Although I didn't have an ending sketched out yet, I hoped this whole new layer of conflict between the brothers would lead me to the right place.

The first night at the cabin the dog got out in the middle of the night and got stuck halfway down the hill, and there was a good deal of searching through underbrush in our pajamas to rescue her. She was barking so loudly it was a homing beacon for every predator within a three-mile radius, and we didn't want to find her carcass picked clean in the morning. It was too steep for us to get down there, and too steep for her to get up, so in the end everyone sat down at the top of the hill and waited for dawn. The stars bowed out, the sky began to brighten, there was the promise of warmth arriving, and then, just before the sun arrived, the dog finally found her own way up the mountain, and we all watched the sunrise together before retreating into the house to make breakfast and start writing.

I don't know if you've been on writing retreats, or if you're in a stage of life where that's possible (certain jobs put a damper on retreats, and so do young children—I know, trust me). But if at all possible, I would encourage you to make time for them. There's an alchemy that happens on the page where mundane thoughts are transformed into glorious prose. You are your best writing self on a retreat. When I was a kid, there was an early Nintendo game called *NBA Jam*, and when the player got hot, the announcer would crow, "He's on fire!" and the basketball would literally be on fire, and no matter where you shot it from, the ball would burn through the net. Being on a writing retreat feels like that. You're on fire. You're en fuego. Nothing can stop you.

I hadn't yet reached the "on fire" part of the writing retreat, but we were only three days in, and I still had confidence that I would get there, and the ending would reveal itself to me. After all, the beginning and the middle of the story were going well, and, more importantly, during the moments when my fingers couldn't type any longer, I was reading a book published by N+1, edited by Chad Harbach, called *MFA/NYC: Two Cultures of American Fiction*. It was basically how to live and make money as a writer.

It's not often you read a book that works like a hinge, and you feel your entire life's orientation swing from one direction to another, but this was a book that did it for me. I realized that for my entire life I'd been living an MFA model of the writing life—you earn spots in prestigious literary journals, publish a highfalutin literary work, then get a tenure track job at a university.

But there was an entirely different way to live as a writer— the NYC model, where you wrote more accessible work and got six-figure advances, and earned money doing freelance writing for magazines, and guest edited and translated and reviewed books and did whatever was necessary to scrape together a living. The MFA model and the university were not working out for me, and it was on this trip I vowed to start living the NYC model. My goal was no longer to get the safe harbor of a teaching job, but to write something that set the world ablaze and earned me fans and deep-pocketed publishers. This was also the book that led me to start working on Bookfox full time, creating online courses for writers.

Now, as far as my own writing, I reached the ending of my story, and I attempted to write it. It didn't work. Now I was stumped. I watched the river, I went running, I talked with my writing friends. Nothing was working. I assembled a lunch, I cooked a late dinner for everyone, and we ate on the porch as the dusky shadows of bats swooped through the filigree of tree branches. That night I changed tack and tried another path for the ending, and when I'd finished, I deleted it all. It was pure rubbish. A good writer must always have a highly sensitive rubbish detector, and delete (no ifs, ands, or buts) when it starts beeping. I went to bed defeated.

In the middle of the night, a sound woke me. It was a shuffling and soft grunting. At first I thought it was in my room—rodent in the rafters or on the floor. But it sounded big, much bigger, and I realized it was coming from outside. I padded to the window and opened the curtain. A gigantic hairy shape lumbered merely feet away, snuffling against the ground. By the light of stars and the faint moon I could barely sketch the outline. It raised a paw and scratched against a tree. My writing companions had told me that the path behind the cabin was a frequently used bear trail, but I hadn't expected to see one, certainly not this close. Perhaps it detected movement at the window, or perhaps it just could feel my eyes on it, so it wheeled and it looked at me. Just for a moment. And then it scampered off, surprisingly light on its feet for something so massive.

I went back to bed feeling the privilege of encountering such a wild animal, and my subconscious did the rest. I woke at dawn and the idea arrived with it. My characters needed to encounter an animal. One of them needed to get bitten, and the wound to get infected. And the ending of the story would be one of the brothers cutting into the puss-filled wound, trying to cut the wound out of his brother to save his life. I went back through the story, setting up the mysterious bite from the beginning, and layering in conversation about it through the middle, all so I could finally write that ending, and I did it.

What's more, I read it and it was good.

We left the Rogue River cabin two days after that and I haven't been back. But the version of the story I wrote up there was published in my story collection—I had finally gotten it right. And I still dream of that cabin sometimes. Not only was it the best and most beautiful writing retreat I've ever gone on, it was also a linchpin moment in my writing life.

Let's arm wrestle a tough subject: ending your chapters. This doesn't get nearly as much attention as the flashier bejeweled topic of the absolute endings of books, the hard-stop, you-better-feel-satisfied-because-there's-no-more type of ending. But your chapter endings have a radical effect on whether your reader finishes your book, so you better believe this linchpin moment deserves a slot in your attention.

But writing a chapter ending resembles the delicate dance of a short story ending, the balance between partial resolution for what's happened so far, and yet simultaneously looking forward to the future. The best way I can describe this is by using a term popularized by Princeton theologian Gerhardus Vos, who described the Kingdom of God as "already, but not yet." It's a delicious phrase. Quite oxymoronic, don't you think?

Your chapter endings need to be "already, but not yet." The "already" part means the endings give emotional or plot satisfaction for what has come before. For instance, you could reference a line earlier in the chapter, which is a technique called a callback, often used by stand-up comedians. A stand-up comedian such as Eddie Izzard references an evil giraffe chewing leaves off trees, miming what this looks like, and then fifteen minutes later in his set, in the middle of a different joke, he mimes the evil giraffe again, which elicits quite a laugh. You can do the same thing in your chapter. A callback makes a chapter feel complete and whole, because it's being bookended by this one small element. You end the chapter by looking backward.

On the other hand, your chapter endings also need to be "not yet." There should be a tease of what is to come. Otherwise your reader is going to close your book and go to bed. The most celebrated version of the "not yet" is a cliffhanger. This is popular for good reason—because it's effective—but sometimes it can feel like the author's using a sledgehammer when a scalpel would be more appropriate. Plus, a cliffhanger can easily become overused, and you risk the reader becoming numb. Ultimately, you need to figure out what the reader wants to look forward to in the story, and to hint at it in the end of the chapter. This part of the chapter ending looks forward.

James McBride is a virtuoso at ending his chapters with an already/not yet technique, especially in his book *The Good Lord Bird*. It's a hilarious book about the abolitionist John Brown and a slave named Onion who spent seventeen years dressed up like a woman, culminating in the historical event of Harper's Ferry. Did I mention it was knee-slappingly funny? It included delightful puns, such as young black men traveling in disguise are "incog-Negro."

Anyhow, for a textbook example of an already/not yet ending, check out chapter 3: "But he made a mistake letting the Reverend go that day, and it would cost him down the line." The "already" part of this sentence looks back at what happened in the chapter—John Brown allows the Reverend to break off from the group, because of a disagreement about freeing slaves. The "not yet" part of this sentence foreshadows what will happen in the future, and we keep turning pages to figure out how it will cost him down the line.

Or this chapter ending: "With that, he turned on his horse and rode off east. I wouldn't see him again for two years." On one hand, we close out the activity of the chapter with one character leaving the other. That's the "already" part, a neat conclusion to the scene. On the other hand, we look forward to the action of the future—what happens two years from now—and we keep reading to see how that next meeting transpires.

In this next chapter ending, all the slaves ready to join their cause at Harper's Ferry have abandoned them and are running away: "I watched the last of them disappear, dodging in and out of the trees, jumping into the thickets, a few sprinting down the tracks, and said, 'We is doomed.'" McBride directs our attention backward, toward the culmination of the chapter as the slaves abandon them, and yet at the same time directs it forward, as Onion realizes their attempt to secure the arsenal at Harper's Ferry will fail.

Too often writers consider plot the only way to create the "not yet" feeling. And if that's the only tool in your writing toolbox, no wonder you start writing 100 percent cliffhangers.

But most writers don't realize the danger of using cliffhangers. I read far too many cliffhanger endings that deliberately manipulate the reader and I can see all the scaffolding of the author. For instance: "And then she knew the identity of the criminal." When I read this, I'm thinking more of the author's technique than I am of the storyline. I know I'm being manipulated. Do I turn the page? Well, probably. Cliffhangers are effective. But I'm taken out of the story. The perfect cliffhanger is one in which the reader doesn't even realize they've been cliffhung (let's pretend that's a word).

If you write cliffhangers, comb through your manuscript and look for ways to soft-pedal it so the reader isn't aware of the authorial hand. The best writer is a magician, making the reader feel the power of the trick but preventing them from noticing the sleight of hand.

Here's an example of a graceful cliffhanger by Ann Patchett, from the ending of her first chapter in *Bel Canto*: "Through the windows, bright red strobe light flashed across the walls accompanied by a high-pitched wailing. The sound was nagging and accusatory. It was nothing, nothing like song."

What's happened in this first chapter is that terrorists have stormed a concert hall and taken everyone hostage. So the chapter ending focuses on the main shift: From song to sirens. From music to wailing. It's a cliffhanger because now that the police have arrived, the reader wants to see what will happen between police and the terrorists. But what makes it graceful?

Well, Patchett doesn't mention the word *police*. That's a small subtlety, but it's important. We just get the sense of the authorities arriving, and of the impending standoff.

Instead of focusing on the faces of police and the bodies of the hostages, Patchett chooses instead to focus only on sound.

What if Patchett had written this as a traditional cliffhanger with all the subtlety of a crowbar? A terrible version might look like this: "At that moment, the police pulled up outside, and we knew the hostilities would begin."

It gets the job done, but it has none of the grace of the authentic version. What's more, her version does a fantastic job of the "already" part of the chapter ending, because this is a chapter that's all about music and sound and singing, and that's reflected in the way she ends the chapter. It looks back with the music and looks forward with how the police will deal with the terrorists.

While a cliffhanger, graceful or not, relies upon *plot* for the tension, I'd recommend using *characters* as the lure that hooks readers and pulls them toward the next chapter.

For instance, in Claire Messud's *The Emperor's Children*, we have a marvelous character-centric book that my book club debated about for five hours in an Italian restaurant in Pasadena (seriously, five hours). When I re-read the book, focusing on chapter endings alone, I noticed that virtually every chapter ends not with plot momentum, but with the deepening of character.

Take chapter 15, for example, where Danielle has just met a man for dinner and there is a flurry of flirtation, and she goes home to think about him:

> And that night, among her Rothkos, Danielle, mint tea in hand, the downtown lights winking knowingly at the window, could not help but remember

that taste, the electricity of him, the charisma, the focus. As if he were alight. And the hand, delicate but firm, not directing but engaging, somehow, a sensation that carried within it, surely not just for her, the promise of something—was it sex? Could it have been?—a promise that she carried away like an unopened present. For next time.

This is such a small movement in her, but it's definitely a change. She's warming up to this man. She's pondering what exactly he's promising her. There's increasing sexual tension between them. And she's already thinking about next time.

How does this work as a chapter ending? Because character change is just as important to the reader as plot development. In fact, in this book, character change is how most of the plot advances. It's satisfying for a reader to witness the forward movement of a person, and curiosity about how this change will affect other characters propels the reader to turn the page.

If you have a huge shift in a character's ideas or perspectives, or even better yet, a character makes a huge decision, that's an excellent place to end a chapter.

I apologize for what I'm going to do to you. After reading this, you'll probably wish that I'd cut this part of the chapter out. Because what I've given you so far is practical, cut-and-dried. You're probably excited to apply the ideas to your chapter endings, and full of optimism and confidence that your chapter endings will be hot-diggity.

But I would be committing literary malpractice if I didn't point out that fiction isn't so neat. For every rule, there are a thousand ways to break that rule. And it's important, I think, for writers to see the full range of possibilities.

I'm going to show you a book that breaks every chapter ending rule we've just talked about. I'm not sure how it works, but it does work, because I love this book.

Check out these seven chapter endings by Haruki Murakami in *The Wind-Up Bird Chronicle*, all of which end with the main character falling asleep. Yes, that's right, the most boring chapter ending possible, and such a terrible ending I might have actually said "Don't do this *ever*," except he has done it, repeatedly, and still created a compulsively readable book. There's not really anything here about "already, but not yet." There's certainly no cliffhanging. He's operating on his own, Murakami-level wavelength.

1. "I fell asleep listening to [the river] flow."

Well, that seems like a natural stopping point.

2. "This time sleep came to take me—a deep sleep that all but pulled me by the ankles to the bottom of the sea."

Not exactly a cliffhanger, is it?

3. "When I went from the bathroom to the bedroom, Kumiko was asleep."

Wow, some real variety, with someone *else* falling asleep this time. Woohoo!

4. "If I shut my eyes, I felt, I would float off somewhere else; I would end up in a wholly different place."

Oh, this chapter ending really changes it up by talking about *not* sleeping.

5. "Then I leaned my head against the wall and closed my eyes. Eventually, sleep overtook me, like a gradually rising tide."

What? How is he pulling this off time and time again? Are you kidding me, Murakami? How many chapters are going to end with sleeping?

6. "He really seemed to be burning himself, I thought. And then I fell asleep."

Is this a practical joke on the reader? How does he make me keep reading?

7. "I stayed up until dawn, unable to sleep. I didn't feel sleepy, for one thing, and in fact, I was afraid to sleep. I had the feeling that if I were to go to sleep, I would be enveloped in a flow of shifting sand that would carry me off to another world, from which I would never be able to return."

How can he get away with ending every chapter with sleep and still create compulsively readable books enjoyed by tens of millions?

Okay, what's our takeaway?

Murakami can make this work because his chapters are already filled with so much excitement and action. So reaching a chapter end feels like a momentary breather, a resting point for the reader, a place to collect themself and orient themself before diving back in. So by crafting the body of the chapters so well, he doesn't need the chapter ending to propel the reader onward. He's coasting off the momentum he's already created.

Plus, falling asleep is thematically powerful in this book. In a book where the protagonist meditates at the bottom of a well, falling asleep is not just falling asleep—it's about falling into a different state of consciousness in order to discover secrets about oneself and the world. Sleeping is a kind of transformative act. So by ending so many of his chapters in a similar way, he's creating a structural unity throughout the book, and reinforcing one of the main themes.

Listen, don't tweak your chapter endings so much that it feels gimmicky, like you're manipulating the reader. End at a natural stopping point. Whatever that point looks like. If you try to game the system too often, it can gum up the works.

Last month I got an email from someone who'd read my book. It's funny—so many writers dream of scoring a huge advance, or having their book made into a movie, or earning a spot on the bestseller list. And I used to dream of those things and believe that I was a failure if I hadn't achieved them. But now I've learned to love the small pleasure of an email from a single reader expressing in heartfelt language that they felt connected to me because of words I put on the page. Honestly, there's nothing better.

This woman said kind things about my book. About what she learned as a writer, about what she enjoyed as a reader. And then she quoted the end of my Indonesia story back to me.

Fellow writers, all that struggle and worry and work and failure, struggling to find that ending, were finally worth it.

WRITING CHALLENGES

1. Go through your manuscript and take out the last paragraph or line from each chapter, putting them all in a new file. Then start to name them, using the techniques here. If you have a technique not listed here, but think you can still identify what you're doing, then write it down. Is there a chapter ending you can't label with a technique? That might be one ripe for revision.

2. Identify how your chapter endings employ the already/not yet tension. Look for ways that the chapter ending looks backward to what's been written, and yet looks forward to what's to come. Revise, trying to include both elements of already/ not yet.

3. Pick out your favorite book and write down the chapter endings for every chapter. How do they keep you reading? Where are they choosing to end their chapters? What is their most effective technique? Is there any similarity to how they end chapters? What techniques can you steal from them?

4. Have a Chapter Ending party. Get together with your writing group and have everyone bring their chapter endings. Study them together. Critique each other's endings. See if you can come up with alternative endings.

5. Write about a writing retreat you've gone on. What did you learn about yourself as a writer? What myths did you dispel? How was it a linchpin moment for

your writing career? And if you haven't gone on a writing retreat, your writing challenge is to plan one.

Further Reading: Google "12 Ways to End a Chapter Bookfox," and you'll find my post with more examples of chapter endings.

9

FINDING AN ENDING

WHEN I TALK TO WRITERS ABOUT THEIR BIGGEST FEARS, they always mention how to end their book. Now I don't mean the climax of the book, I'm talking about the absolute last paragraph, the coda to the entire story. This is the way you ease the reader out from the dream of the book and push them back into the real world, with your story still lingering on their brain. It's not easy. There's a huge amount of pressure on that final paragraph, nearly as much as on the first paragraph. It's a paragraph where you either leave your mark on the reader or you stumble and fumble.

Now, in my book club we particularly love endings. In fact, we have voted on our favorite endings out of the nearly eighty books we've read together over the last fifteen years. Because I like you, I'm going to share my book club's three favorite endings and give some tips about the linchpin moment of your ending.

If you couldn't tell, it's quite a serious book club. We take vacations together to the places where the books are set, like New Orleans (Walker Percy's *The Moviegoer* and *A Confederacy of Dunces* by John Kennedy Toole) and to Palm Springs (*Generation X* by Douglas Coupland), and read those books out loud in the city where they were written. We have strict rules about how each member gets to play the dictator and choose the book for that round, and we only read fiction, preferably fiction without a page count so high it could induce a nose bleed.

And, yes, we tailor the food and drink to the book we're reading. For Cormac McCarthy's *Blood Meridian* we served hardscrabble man-food like nuts and salami. For Madeline Miller's *Circe* we did a very Greek thing and drank wine from bowls (yes, ceramic bowls). For Han Kang's *The Vegetarian* we ate South Korean snacks like dried squid, dried cuttlefish, and Hite beer.

We call ourselves the Bookhouse Boys, inspired by the secret society in the television series *Twin Peaks*, and, yes, we've even made little pins with a tree bisected by a sword (super geeky, I know). We're not one of those groups that talks about the book for ten minutes and then gossips for the next two hours. No, we really devote ourselves to deep discussion about every title for at least two hours, sometimes three.

This is the extent of our devotion: when the COVID pandemic hit, and all in-person meetings were canceled, we refused to let it to disrupt our sacred gathering. Instead of our normal meeting location at my house, we met in the parking lot of the courthouse, where we parked our cars like spokes and sat in beach chairs in a gigantic circle, ten feet between each of us. Oh, and the first time we met it was raining. We had to use umbrellas to shield ourselves and our books. You know what? It was the most memorable meeting we've ever had. During quarantine we had seven meetings in a parking lot, because nothing, not even a pandemic, is going to stop us talking about books.

We've even had an ongoing bet that one of our members, who'd started a popular podcast, would interview the notoriously reclusive Cormac McCarthy or else he would play a fiddle naked while dancing on a table (yes, this is a *Blood Meridian* reference). Our friend still maintains that since McCarthy hasn't died yet, it's still possible for him to win the bet. But I'm betting on some naked fiddling.

My favorite part about my book club is that none of the others are writers. I spent decades of my life talking about fiction with other writers, and while it was rewarding, it also warped my writing. Unconsciously, I started writing to please other writers rather than writing to please regular readers. This is a bear trap, because the vast majority of readers aren't writers, and so if you're talking explicitly to them, you're seriously limiting your audience. With my book club, I get to hear what salesmen, lawyers, teachers, and philosophers think about the book, which is wonderfully insightful and keeps me grounded.

If you don't have a book club yet, it's time for you to start one. There's nothing like a book club to create a community that values the written word. Also, when you strongly disagree with someone else about the selected book, and end up in a shouting match punctuated by copious amounts of swearing, and some spittle flies out and lands on their shirt, and some drinks get spilled, and both of you are slightly drunk, and it becomes so heated you have to apologize by the end, you can't help but lie in bed that night and think: *Damn, books matter.*

Of course that's a purely hypothetical situation. Totally. Never happened. Nope. But what shouldn't be hypothetical is you sending an email to four of your friends tonight recommending that you start up a book club. It will fuel your writing in ten thousand subtle ways.

So because of our club's ardent devotion, you might be curious about our favorite ending. Out of the eighty books we've read together, what is our favorite ending, the one that stuck with us the most? And when we voted, and tallied everything up on a handy spreadsheet, it was no contest. There was one book far above the rest, one book that we all agreed had the best ending perhaps ever written. It was a classic: Steinbeck's *The Grapes of Wrath*.

In this bleak story of poverty and farming during the Great Depression, Steinbeck ends the book with a problem: the Joads have found a starving man in a barn. He hasn't had food in five days. The Joads have no food to offer him, but one of them, Rose of Sharon, who had recently given birth to a stillborn baby, knows what she has to do:

> For a minute Rose of Sharon sat still in the whispering barn. Then she hoisted her tired body up and drew the comfort about her. She moved slowly to the corner and stood looking down at the wasted face, into the wide, frightened eyes. Then slowly she lay down beside him. He shook

his head slowly from side to side. Rose of Sharon loosened one side of the blanket and bared her breast. "You got to," she said. She squirmed closer and pulled his head close. "There!" she said. "There." Her hand moved behind his head and supported it. Her fingers moved gently in his hair. She looked up and across the barn, and her lips came together and smiled mysteriously.

It is one of the most gracious acts that one could imagine. In a book where the women are the heroes and the men are selfish louts, the book ends on a sacrificial act from the teenage Rose of Sharon as she breastfeeds a grown man to save him from starvation. There are echoes of the Madonna in a scene such as this, as Mary was often portrayed with Baby Jesus suckling from her. And the substitutionary act is hard to miss, because even though Rose of Sharon's baby has died, her body, full of milk, can still nourish someone else.

After reading a book where the adults frequently can't feed their children, where pigs eat a human baby, where a whole menagerie of animals die, where a family loses their home and become homeless migrants traipsing across a dust bowl of a country, where a group of people called Okies are discriminated against and harassed, and where the employers abuse every worker, this final act stands in sharp contrast. After such pain comes succor. After such hardship comes comfort. This ending serves as a contrast to what has come before, and yet also continues the theme of hunger.

Our second favorite ending came from Douglas Coupland's *Generation X*, a book so seismic it ended up naming a generation. This is a book where three twenty-somethings try to find meaning in their lives. The characters search for experiences that will help them justify their existence, and they keep failing to find it. Until the end.

Andy, driving near the Salton Sea in California, witnesses a thermonuclear cloud, and he imagines the world is ending. He pulls over to watch but discovers it's only a gigantic smoke cloud from farmers burning their fields. Then a "cocaine white egret" starts flying over the burnt fields, ends up dive bombing him and scratching his head, and he starts bleeding. A group of Down syndrome preteens takes pity on his bloodied head and surrounds him, trying to comfort him:

> Then, from behind me I felt another pair of hands as one of her friends joined in. Then another pair. Suddenly I was dog-piled by an instant family, in their adoring, healing, uncritical embrace, each member wanting to show their affection more than the other. They began to hug me—too hard— as though I *were* a doll, unaware of the strength they exerted. I was being winded—crushed— pinched and trampled.
>
> The man with the beard came over to yank them away. But how could I explain to him, this well-intentioned gentleman, that this discomfort, no this *pain*, I was experiencing was no problem at all, that in fact, this crush of love was unlike anything I had ever known.

Andy has been searching for a family for the entire book, searching for acceptance and community, and here, in the embrace of these preteens, he finally finds it. This is uncritical love that embraces him unconditionally.

Our third favorite book ending came from Jay McInerney's *Bright Lights, Big City*. The narrator has been hopped up on cocaine for a good portion of the book (amusingly, he calls it "Bolivian marching powder"). By the end of the book, his girlfriend has broken up with him and gotten engaged to someone else, his mother has recently died, and he's lost his job. His nose is bleeding, he's hungover, and he can barely walk. He's stumbling around New York City when he smells freshly baked bread. And small note: It's told in the second person, so "you" instead of "I."

> You get down on your knees and tear open the bag. The smell of warm dough envelops you. The first bite sticks in your throat and you almost gag. You will have to go slowly. You will have to learn everything all over again.

I love the hope of this ending. Yes, he's on his knees, both figuratively and literally, and had to beg for bread from a tattooed dock loader. But the arc of his story, we hope, will start to point up, because he's determined to start over and learn everything again.

The bread is such a powerful symbol. A page earlier, he links freshly baked bread with his recently deceased mother and remembers how he used to come in the kitchen while she was baking. So the bread is a way of remembering her, and remembering that her death was what sent him into the downward spiral. Bread also serves as a communion meta-phor. This notion of starting again and being reborn while eating bread has strong religious overtones. For him, this is the bread of life.

It alludes to a famous short story ending by Raymond Carver in "A Small, Good Thing," in which parents grieving over the death of their son confront a baker for harassing them over the phone, and he apologizes and feeds them bread as a way to help them manage their grief. The bread is a small, good thing—a reminder that tiny acts of graciousness are essential when experiencing tragedy.

All three of these endings are happy, and yet all three are cut with an element of sadness—it's sad that Rose of Sharon has to breastfeed a man to save him from starvation, and painful that Andy is bleeding from the egret's talons, and the "You" of *Bright Lights, Big City* is really scraping the bottom of his life. A happy ending that is 100 percent happy ends up being unpalatably sweet. If you're going to end on some uplifting note, it should be bittersweet in some way. Lace that happiness with an element of pain.

All three of these endings are also beginnings. They open up to the character's future. For Rose of Sharon and the Joads, it gives us hope that they will get through the Great Depression by radical acts of generosity and sacrifice. For Andy, perhaps this experience of unconditional love will help him stop searching for acceptance. And for the "You" narrator of *Bright Lights, Big City*, we have hope that's he's going to turn his life around, stop using drugs, stop partying so hard, and learn how to live again.

To nail the linchpin moment of an ending, your goal should be to develop a philosophy of endings. I'm not going to waggle my finger while lecturing you on the correct philosophy, but the wider range of endings you've experienced, the better sense you'll have for your own ending.

It should be a personal philosophy—what do you think an ending should do for the reader? You get to decide how to end your book, and there are so many choices you have. And your philosophy of endings should be broad enough to accommodate for different books. When I look over an author's oeuvre, I find that they often tilt to a particular type of ending in multiple books, which means that authors have an instinct about it, whether formally sketched out or not, that leads them to write similar endings.

I once emailed a woman who had taken my online writing courses, and we were talking about endings. I told her that her ending didn't quite work. I recommended an alternative ending, one that made the main character more active. She countered that she wanted to keep it the same because she wanted to make a point that sometimes you do everything and fail, and then it still works out for you. So I said if she wanted to do that style of ending, she should study some stories that ended in a similar manner. I recommended reading *The Alchemist* by Paulo Coelho, a short fable that ends in a similar manner. She emailed back to say that she had read it, twice, and she hated that ending. Then she conceded that perhaps she *should* change the ending.

This anecdote shows the importance of identifying endings that you *don't* want to write. Start creating a list now. What endings have you hated? You should catalogue them and examine them to help you decide what type of endings to avoid.

For instance, the last ten pages of Donna Tartt's *The Goldfinch* explain the whole novel. The ending is completely undramatic, although it does paint a thick varnish of meaning onto the book. I could easily see an author reading that and saying: *I will never write this style of ending.*

Or consider an ending like the one in Yann Martel's *The Life of Pi*, which makes you doubt the veracity of the entire novel (*Were they animals in that boat or were they people?*). This type of ending is a trick—do you want to undermine the reader's expectations of your book in that way?

These are questions that you can answer only after you've read these books and had the emotional experience of their endings. You have to develop an unerring instinct for your type of endings. But in the end, be willing to break your rules if the book requires it.

Now let's highlight four other types of endings that don't get as much attention, probably because they're harder to pull off.

A **Descriptive Ending** doesn't involve the main characters and it's often focused on describing the natural world. Cormac McCarthy pulls this off in *The Road*:

> Once there were brook trout in streams in the mountains. You could see them standing in the amber current where the white edges of their fins wimpled softly in the flow. They smelled

of moss in your hand. Polished and muscular and torsional. On their backs were vermiculate patterns that were maps of the world in its becoming. Maps and mazes. Of a thing which could not be put back. Not be made right again. In the deep glens where they lived all things were older than man and they hummed of mystery.

You don't always have to end on character or plot. A descriptive ending like this works because McCarthy makes us feel three things.

First, I'm slightly *jealous* at McCarthy's command of language, filled both with words I had to look up (*vermiculate*: "marked with irregular fine lines") and words that I admire (*wimpled*, *glens*, *hummed*). At the same time, he makes me feel *nostalgic* for this type of unsullied environment. Even though we haven't yet lost the beauty of our natural world, after steeping yourself in the ashy wrecked world of the novel, you'll want to preserve it more than ever. Lastly, I feel *wonder* very strongly when I read this passage. I'm marveling at the glories of a trout's body, and the way a trout's body is a microcosm for the mysteries of the world.

Gabriel Garcia Marquez's book *Love in the Time of Cholera*, uses a **Dialogue Ending**. It ends on dialogue—a single word of dialogue. This book, about the delay of love, shows how this couple kept their affection alive for the fifty-three years they were apart. And then he's asked, at the end, how long he can keep up the love: "'Forever,' he said."

A dialogue ending works well because you're giving your main character the chance to cast one last spell over the book. This single word works like a promise, the equivalent of an "I do" at the altar. It also references time, because although they've been separated for half a century, that time pales in light of the time he vows to spend with her in the future, a virtual eternity.

With a dialogue ending, attempt to pick a short phrase that encapsulates some essential element of the book.

A **Plot Ending** concludes with a further twist of the plot. For instance, in Elmore Leonard's book *The Switch*, we don't really understand the title until the very last few pages of the book. In the book, a group of criminals kidnap a man's wife and hold her for ransom, threatening to kill her if he doesn't pony up a million dollars cash. Unfortunately for the kidnappers, the husband was about to divorce his wife. He would actually prefer if they knock her off, because it would save him all the alimony.

So at the end of the book, the wife joins the kidnappers to kidnap the mistress instead, in order to extract the million dollars out of her husband. When the mistress walks out of the bathroom, she sees everyone masked up, ready to abduct her: "There were three Richard Nixons sitting by the coffee table." And the mistress doesn't even realize what's happening to her, doesn't yet realize she's about to be kidnapped. The last line of the book shows the wife thinking that she wants to go home and watch the expression on her husband's face as he gets this new ransom call, a ransom call for his mistress, a ransom that he'll actually have to pay.

Another way to think about this ending is that it ends with a surprise. What is one final twist you can offer that will give the reader pleasure?

Consider the ending of Margaret Atwood's novel *The Handmaid's Tale*, which features a **Question Ending**.

A question ending is excellent because it reflects the book back onto the reader, as if asking them to respond now that they're finished. And it also opens the book outward. The long series of declarative phrases are over, and now it's time to ponder and respond to the question posed.

In fact, a question ending works so well I decided to use it for the ending of this book. (Don't look ahead! You'll ruin the surprise.)

But now I've kept you waiting, and I might as well sign off for this chapter by revealing the last line of Atwood's book. This ending comes after we've seen all the horrible ways that the government of Gilead has treated women, reducing them to incubators for babies. And the last chapter of the book jumps far into the future, where a historian looks back on the characters in the book and talks about what made their lives so miserable. The last line is asked by the academic to the members of the audience, but it doubles as a question for the reader, asking them whether they want to live in a world where they have enough freedom to make an inquiry:

"Are there any questions?"

WRITING CHALLENGES

1. Create a list of five books whose endings you've hated. What did you dislike about them?
2. Create a list of three of your favorite endings and why they were fantastic.
3. Write a personal philosophy of endings. This should be written as a manifesto, with a list of firm declarations and resolute convictions about what you think an ending should and shouldn't do. If you have written some endings before, cite your own endings in making your case.

Further Reading: Google "Why Writers Need a Book Club (and 21 Tips to Make It Great!)" to learn more about how to create your own book club.

10

SURPRISE ME!

EVERY WRITER NEEDS TO KNOW THE DIFFERENCE BETWEEN mystery and anticipation.

Mystery is if I told you, "You might or might not have a huge writing success this year. Read the rest of this book to find out." Assuming you don't torture me for not telling you right away, wouldn't you want to keep reading to figure out the details of that success? That mystery propels you through the book.

And that's why most writers default to the technique of mystery. They figure if they keep holding all their narrative cards close to their chest, the reader will keep playing the game of reading to peek at those cards. But I've seen this technique backfire hundreds of times in novels, especially when you don't give the reader enough information, or the narrator is withholding capriciously, or you don't steadily reveal more and more information. And even in popular culture, I see mystery abused as a form in shows like *Lost* and *Westworld*, where it reduces the story to an algebraic problem, a puzzle to be solved rather than a story with emotional resonance.

Anticipation, on the other hand, would be if I said, "A publisher will offer you a $250,000 advance for your book on October 13 of this year, and you will receive the news at two in the afternoon, moments before you start spelunking in a cave in Patagonia." All the most important information is there! I've tried to be as frank and detailed and revealing as possible. You already know the ending, and yet you still want to keep reading. You want to know what book you've written, perhaps, or what publisher is crazy enough to give you that kind of moolah, or why in the world you'd be in Patagonia entering a cave when you have a deathly fear of bats?

Gabriel Garcia Marquez uses the preemptive strike of anticipation in his book *Chronicle of a Death Foretold*. Jeez, Marquez, you can't even wait until the first line to give away the ending? Nope, the gabby guy reveals it right in the title. Or in *The Lovely Bones*, Alice Sebold uses anticipation when the narrator tells you on the first page that she is dead and looking down from heaven. But in both these books, you keep reading because you want to know *how* it occurs. Every reader wants the juicy details.

Far fewer beginning writers use the technique of anticipation, probably because they underestimate how powerfully it hooks the reader and keeps them reading, but in many aspects it's easier to pull off than mystery. For instance, the beginning of this chapter uses the strategy of anticipation in a nonfiction way—I tell you my main point, and you keep reading to figure out what I mean.

Both mystery and anticipation have something in common: they both end with the element of surprise. With mystery, the surprise is discovering the ending: every one of the bandits dies; a team of thieves succeeds in stealing money in a bank heist; a couple must decide whether or not to divorce. With anticipation, on the other hand, the surprise is *how* the ending happens: yes, the bandits all die, because one of their own betrays them; yes, the heist happens, but they end up getting robbed by someone else; yes, a couple divorces, but their divorce lawyers end up marrying each other.

Now, why did I put this chapter in the "Endings" section? Because a surprise is actually an ending, the ending of a plot. The beginning is when the writer creates a mystery or makes you anticipate the end, and the surprise is the conclusion. Remember that this technique doesn't only work in terms of the huge, big-picture plot. You don't only get one surprise per book. This use of surprise can happen on a paragraph level as well.

Ultimately, whether you use mystery or anticipation as the main way you coax the reader through your book, you still need to nail the surprise. And that's what this chapter is going to help you with.

Tania Luna was one year old, living in Ukraine, when the Chernobyl nuclear reactor exploded. It rained black, her sister lost all her hair, and Tania spent nine months in a hospital with no visitors allowed (because of radiation fears). Thankfully, there was an upside to the disaster: when she turned six, her family received asylum in the United States.

In the United States, they lived below the poverty line, struggling to survive, but since she was so young, she didn't even realize the extent of their poverty. Her stuffed animals and bike were dug out of a dumpster, they lived in a homeless shelter for a while, and even buying a piece of Bazooka bubble gum was a celebratory event. On top of all that, her parents divorced.

Given that tumultuous upbringing, it's understandable that Tania tried to avoid surprises. She wanted the predictable. She wanted safety. Things that were unexpected were to be avoided—they were dangerous. But as she grew up and got settled, her life started to feel stale. She and her husband were middle class, safe, and a little bored. Something had to change.

That's when she decided that she needed to artificially create surprises in her life. Her personal attempts of interrupting her patterns went so well that she decided to create surprises for others as well. She started a company called Surprise Industries, which creates surprises for teams and individuals, wrote a book about surprises, and started calling herself a "surprisologist." Now she stands on stages waving glow sticks and orchestrating surprises for groups, such as a person in a chicken suit leading a full auditorium in a dance party.

She has seen firsthand how surprising people enriches their lives, and that a life without surprises is dull. And this isn't just anecdotal experience—the salutary benefit of surprises is well documented by scientific research.

In her book, she writes, "When we are surprised, our emotions intensify up to 400 percent." After all, studies have shown that monkeys experience much more dopamine from unexpected rewards than from expected ones. Want to deliver a big load of dopamine to a reader? Simply surprise them. In her talk for TEDx, she said, "Surprise hijacks all our mental processes . . . and pulls our focus onto one thing, onto the thing that surprised us." And then our brains become "wildly curious" to figure out why we've been so surprised.

Tania has done the research that shows us exactly why surprises work so well, not only in our personal lives to keep us feeling alive and fully present, but also in our books. Now let's figure out how to use surprises in your writing.

Let's be honest: you need small surprises in your book. You can find a good book without a huge, groundbreaking surprise in it, but it's rare to find a book without any type of surprise at all. Without some element of surprise, a book feels workmanlike, plodding along with any emotional peaks and valleys for the reader. With a surprise, you can shock the reader and make them sit up a little straighter, and that's why a surprise is one of the linchpin scenes in your book.

So you should be planning surprises from the beginning, although many surprises rise organically through the writing process. After all, it was Robert Frost who said, "No surprise for the writer, no surprise for the reader." If a narrative twist surprises you, there's a much better chance it will surprise the reader.

Now this is a surprise so famous you all know it, a surprise that doesn't feel surprising but which was a shock for the first readers of Frank Baum back in 1900 when the book was first published. Dorothy and Toto and her three friends return to the Wizard of Oz to claim what he promised them—brain, heart, courage, and a trip back home—and discover things are not quite as they seem:

> The Lion thought it might be as well to frighten the Wizard, so he gave a large, loud roar, which was so fierce and dreadful that Toto jumped away from him in alarm and tipped over the screen that stood in a corner. As it fell with a crash they looked that way, and the next moment all of them were filled with wonder. For they saw, standing in just the spot the screen had hidden, a little old man, with a bald head and a wrinkled face, who seemed to be as much surprised as they were. The Tin Woodman, raising his axe, rushed toward the little man and cried out, "Who are you?"
>
> "I am Oz, the Great and Terrible," said the little man, in a trembling voice. "But don't strike me—please don't—and I'll do anything you want me to."

This surprise works because Frank Baum has spent the entire book preparing the reader for the opposite, making us believe that the Wizard is truly a great wizard.

- Witch of the North: "Oz himself is the Great Wizard. . . . He is more powerful than all the rest of us together. He lives in the City of Emeralds."
- Little Old Woman: "It is exactly in the center of the country, and is ruled by Oz, the Great Wizard I told you of."
- A man: "You see, Oz is a Great Wizard, and can take on any form he wishes."
- Munchkin-sized man: "Oz is powerful and terrible, and if you come on an idle or foolish errand to bother the wise reflections of the Great Wizard, he might be angry and destroy you all in an instant."
- The greatness of the Emerald City and the multiple soldiers belonging to the Guardians of the Gate make us think that this wizard must indeed be very powerful.
- The whole book is aimed toward the Wizard of Oz, so the story structure makes us believe he's the answer to their problems.

In the end, this type of surprise only works when you've spent the entire novel making the reader believe the opposite. The more you build up expectations in one direction, the higher level of surprise when you reverse course and reveal that the opposite is true.

There's always a tension between laying the foundation too securely for your surprise, so the reader sees it coming, and not preparing the reader enough, in which case they don't buy the plot twist. If you prepare the reader too much, it's anticlimactic when you finally get to the surprise. You've tipped your hand. They've guessed the surprise. On the other hand, if you don't prepare the reader enough, in subtle and unconscious ways, for this development, then they won't buy it.

In a similar vein—a huge, book-ending surprise—we can look at Edwidge Danticat's *The Dew Breaker*, where we've been learning about a character's father and mother for the whole novel. We know that the father was a torturer in Haiti during the Duvalier dictatorship, and that he married the mother without telling her about his past. And yet at the very end of the book, we see the details of how he met the mother: he ran away from the prison, bleeding from his face because one of the people he was torturing cut him, and the mother assumed he was one of the tortured, not the torturer. It's a shocking moment for the reader. Their entire relationship was based on a misunderstanding. She married him because she thought he was a victim, but the truth was that he was the oppressor.

What kind of surprise is this? It's a surprise by omission, not like the direct deception in *The Wizard of Oz*. We had assumed one thing about the relationship of this couple, and it turned out there was a secret, and it was shocking. It's lovely because we didn't even know there was more to that story, but what we had assumed to be true ended up being a distortion.

For a completely different type of surprise, let's look at surprises *after* the climax. Normally, after the main climax has occurred, readers are ready to pack it in. Story's over, let's turn off the lights and call it a night. And that's a perfect opportunity for a writer—readers aren't expecting a huge surprise, not in this moment of calm.

Let's go retro and haul out Homer's *Odyssey*. Yep, when looking at storytelling structures, you can't get better than the Greeks. This is a book where the entire story involves Odysseus trying to get home, and so naturally we expect the book to be wrapping up when, after his cunning defeat of the lotus-eaters and sirens and cyclops and witches and cannibals and six-headed monsters, he *finally* reaches home.

But not so fast! The surprise twist is that he's been away so long that nobody believes it's him, not even his wife. So now he has a new mission to assert his identity as the true king and prove he's not an imposter.

Or think about the end of *The Lord of the Rings* trilogy, in the book *The Return of the King*. After the ring has been destroyed and Sauron defeated and the huge battle with the Army of Mordor, the story's over, right? Well, actually Frodo and the hobbits return home only to discover hoodlums have set up a mafia enterprise in the Shire, and they have to fight to regain their old neighborhood. It's a surprising twist that the battle isn't quite over, and that the huge battle in faraway lands has come home to roost in their tiny corner of the world.

Peter Jackson left this part out of the film because he never liked this ending, but I feel like he's missing that Tolkien was trying to describe the emotions of soldiers returning home from WWI and finding that everything had changed in their absence. (But maybe it's better Jackson dropped it, because the director's cut is already *eleven hours*.)

On a different note, I've also seen writers deliver a type of surprise at the end of the chapter. I think of these as little rewards for the reader, like party favors for coming to their book. And these surprises aren't always huge plot developments (although cliffhangers often can be surprising).

For instance, in *The Book of Strange New Things*, Michel Faber uses a fascinating anticipation technique for each chapter: the title of each chapter is the last sentence in the chapter. So when the chapter is called "Take a Deep Breath and Count to a Million," the reader wonders for the entire chapter: How will events play out so we can reach a scene where that line makes sense as the last sentence? Another chapter is called "He Realized for the First Time That She Was Beautiful, Too." So the reader wonders: Who is she? What event gives him this epiphany that she's beautiful? The surprise happens when we reach the end of the chapter and discover it's not what we had expected.

Another example of anticipation and surprise at the end of a section is in *Cloud Atlas* by David Mitchell. The structure of this book is quite fascinating—it's built like a Russian nesting doll. So the first part tells the first half of stories 1 through 6, and the second part tells the second half of the stories, starting at story 6 and going back to 1. And these stories differ wildly in terms of place and time, spanning from a dystopian future with slave clones in Korea to Belgium in the early 1900s.

In each section, we learn how the character discovers the writing or recording of the character in the next section. For instance, a vanity publisher named Timothy Cavendish reads a manuscript that is the story of the previous character. And one character, before he takes his own life, mails the letters of another storyline to a friend. So in each section of the book, the reader starts anticipating how the storylines will connect. In what way will the characters run across the other stories, in written or verbal form? How will they discover them? It's a surprise we know is coming, but in every section it's still a surprise we look forward to, as we suss out the thin strand that ties these disparate stories together.

Side surprises are equally important in your book. Side surprises are surprises that are not essential for the book's core story, but kind of a collateral surprise.

P. D. James, in *The Children of Men*, imagines a world in which everyone has gone infertile, and there haven't been any children born for the last twenty-five years. In a world such as this, doll makers have been a booming industry, because mothers have been frustrated by their infertility and have started pushing around strollers with dolls inside. Inside that world, there's a small incident the narrator witnesses. As a woman pushes a stroller, he sees a second woman stop, pretend to examine the fake baby in the carriage, and then the story takes a wholly unexpected turn: "The second woman suddenly seized the doll, tore it from the coverings and, without a word, swung it twice round her head by the legs and dashed it against the stone wall with tremendous force. The face shattered and shards of porcelain fell tinkling to the pavement."

Even though it's only a doll, we're still horrified by this act of cruelty, and the "mother" starts wailing inconsolably. This incident doesn't further the plot in any way, and it doesn't directly involve one of our main characters. It's more of a side surprise, an event that helps the reader understand the alternative universe of the novel.

Those are the surprises that come inside the book, but don't forget about surprises outside the book: the surprises of your writing life. For most writers, we think we know what the biggest surprises will be. We think it'll be winning that contest or getting a book published or landing on the bestseller list or getting that glowing review or reading the email announcing we've won that huge prize.

But the biggest surprises in your writing life often come from inside you, as a seismic shift in your perspective allows you to do something you could never do before. In this way, I'd argue that the most surprising things are—surprise, surprise—things that we don't see coming at all. For instance:

Perhaps you were hesitant to write a book because it seemed crazy or unmarketable, but you surprise yourself by writing it anyway, and it's this book that is your breakthrough.

You stop believing that you're stupid, or that you're unbelievably smart, and accept your role as a writer—a role that is more delightful than you'd anticipated or less star-studded than your fantasy, but which gives you enormous fulfilment.

You start to find pleasure in the act of writing itself, rather than only looking forward to what happens after the writing.

You're asked to cowrite a book, or ghostwrite a book, or write a book outside your genre, or build a writing business, or become a book editor, or become a book reviewer, or become an agent, or start a publishing house. And more importantly, you believe you can actually do it.

You stop being scared of what other people will think about your writing, and write with a devil-may-care attitude, only listening to your own counsel.

And surprise! Happy birthday! Get jiggy with it and blow out some candles. You've been reborn as a writer.

WRITING CHALLENGES:

1. Write a five-hundred-word story that has a huge surprise in the last line.
2. Find a place where you've written either a mystery or used the technique of anticipation. Rewrite that story using the opposite technique. How does it change the tension of the narrative? Does it work better the original way or the revised way?
3. Write a minor surprise into your work-in-progress. It doesn't have to be part of the main plot, just a side surprise that a character witnesses that dovetails nicely with the themes of the book. For instance, if you have a book with themes of hunger or deprivation, you could show a character stumbling into a competitive-eating competition at a fair.
4. Write a few paragraphs about your biggest doubts or fears as a writer. Then pretend one of your writer friends told you he had these same doubts/fears. What counsel would you give him?

11

HOW TO KILL YOUR CHARACTERS

A BRITISH AUTHOR OF A SERIES DECIDED HE WAS TIRED OF writing about his famous character. He thought this character was getting in the way of his literary development and wanted time to write other stories. So he decided to kill his character, hoping it would end one stage of his writing career and usher in a new one.

He wrote a final story where the character's nemesis lured him to Switzerland, and they fought in hand-to-hand combat until they both fell over Reichenbach Falls to their deaths. The name of the story couldn't be mistaken for playing coy: it was called "The Final Problem" and opened with the line "It is with a heavy heart that I take up my pen to write these, the last words . . ."

This story was published in *The Strand Magazine* in 1893 and was met with immediate uproar. A deluge of 20,000 readers protested by canceling their subscriptions to the magazine, and some young men in London wore black crepes on their hats and arms for more than a month as a sign of mourning. In fact, the author became depressed from the overwhelming number of angry letters he received, with former fans opening letters with salutations like, "You brute!"

The author, as you might have guessed with elementary ease, was Sir Arthur Conan Doyle, and his newly deceased character was Sherlock Holmes. In the end, the public outcry was so great Doyle was forced to resurrect his famous detective by explaining away his supposed death and giving him a new case to solve.

This is a cautionary tale about how *not* to kill a character.

First, Doyle had a motivation that lay outside the realm of the story. It wasn't that Sherlock Holmes had run up against the end of his adventures, it was that Doyle was tired of writing him. The death was more about Doyle's ambitions than it was about Sherlock Holmes, and that's always a recipe for error.

Second, Doyle didn't quite realize that by sharing his character with the world, the character became part of the fabric of his readers' lives. So even though he felt completely unemotional about knocking off his most famous literary creation, he hadn't taken into account how his fans might feel. The story came off as calloused; he had misjudged his audience (he also misjudged his career—can you name any other stories or characters written by Doyle?).

Third, Doyle was writing a serialized story in which episodic mysteries occurred, and he hadn't built up properly to a climactic point in which it made sense for the protagonist to die. If you kill your main character, the story has to demand it.

Despite Sir Arthur Conan Doyle's misstep in killing Sherlock Holmes, it actually can be a wise move to kill off characters in your book, and consider this chapter a primer in how to kill one (or more) properly.

Why is killing a character generally a good move? Well, because it's something I call an emotional cattle prod. Certain elements in fiction always goad your readers into feeling something—weddings, engagements, sex, births, divorces, illnesses, deaths. These are all events that readers latch onto easily, instinctively relate to, and which provoke strong emotion. (To learn more about emotional cattle prods, take my "Write Your Best Novel" course.)

If you want to see a landscape festooned with emotional cattle prods, watch soap operas. Every episode includes at least a few, and that's because the writers know that if they stuff enough of them in the narrative, the writing doesn't have to be good. The viewer transposes their personal lives onto the lives of the characters, and they can't stop watching. They can't stop watching because they can't stop feeling. These emotional cattle prods zap the viewer with bursts of dopamine, and the viewer gets addicted to that kind of storytelling.

I had a friend, Jaime Taite, who played a secretary called Hillary in the famous soap opera series, *The Bold and the Beautiful*. In her first day of filming, there was a sex scandal, betrayal, blackmail, a character who'd slept with his girlfriend's mother, a case of mistaken identity, and a termination of employment. Yep, that was a *single* episode.

Now, I'm not recommending you write soap operas. But like every other genre, soap operas can teach us. Soap operas know how to manipulate others by storytelling. And though as a writer you don't want manipulate in a pejorative sense, you do want to massage your story to create the biggest dramatic effect on the reader. You should be inserting emotional cattle prods like death into your story—meaning, don't exhaust your reader with tragedies and celebrations on every page, but do use them periodically to zap your reader with emotional fervor.

Although soap operas go too far into the realm of the melodramatic, literary fiction can wander too far into the realm of the everyday. If you have thirty pages in which there's not a single dramatic event, that's a good sign you might want to draw some inspiration from soap operas and jolt your readers with some kind of cattle prod. Such as a death.

I promise you this: if you kill a major character in your book, that will be the first and sometimes only thing your reader will remember five or ten years after reading your book. Death is simply that memorable. And that's what makes death a linchpin moment in your book.

The patron saint of character murders, the absolute cardinal of character killing, the unabashed doyen of death, is George R. R. Martin. In his *Game of Thrones* series, Martin uses character killing as a way to manage his relationship with readers:

> I've been killing characters my entire career, maybe I'm just a bloody minded bastard, I don't know. When my characters are in danger, I want you to be afraid to turn the page. [The author] needs to show right from the beginning that you're playing for keeps.

Martin wants to keep the reader honest, to hook the reader's attention by keeping all options on the table, and to raise the stakes. His greatest fear is that the reader will grow complacent.

In most polite fiction, there is an unspoken contract with the reader that beloved characters won't be offed; it's called "plot armor." These are characters essential for the storyline, and so they're immune to death. Unfortunately, plot armor reduces the tension for readers because they know one of their greatest fears—that their favorite character will die—isn't going to happen. But with Martin, you know he doesn't play by those parlor rules. Nothing is off the table. Which makes you, as a reader, more curious about how the story will unroll, because the story lanes have had the kid bumpers removed.

So in *Game of Thrones*, when the honorable patriarch of the family, Ned Stark, gets executed in the first book, we start to understand that this is a fictional world without the traditional constraints. And later in the series, when we're at a joyous wedding celebration, we see three main characters—characters that we've grown to love, characters we thought were the future of the series—get brutally murdered, and now all bets are off for how this story will play out.

People have complained about the high body count of Martin, as if he's some brave pioneer of snuffing out characters en masse, but I'd like to bring up another author whose body count dwarfs his, an author you might have heard of: Shakespeare. At least 155 characters die in his 38 plays, from protagonists to antagonists to deuteragonists. You're not a real Shakespeare character unless you've died or your friend has died or your parents have died. So Martin's macabre focus isn't all that unusual, it's just that we've become a little soft in our expectations that our beloved characters will reach the safe harbor of the final page.

Cormac McCarthy kills his characters for an entirely different reason than Martin does. His character deaths are not managing the reader's expectations but showcasing the way he views the universe. McCarthy wants to highlight the true face of evil in his books, and the high body count is the natural result of that evil.

In *Blood Meridian*, McCarthy kneecaps the reader with a litany of deaths, including indiscriminate slaughter of Native Americans, dead babies hung from a tree, and Judge Holden's death-hug of the kid in the outhouse. With each of these three he is making a specific point about these deaths. The slaughter of Native Americans shows McCarthy trying to invert our rosy history and point out the bloodthirsty genocide committed by early settlers. With the dead babies he's pointing out the inhumanity of humans to each other and the depths to which we will sink. And with Judge Holden, who is a hairless, erudite, seven-foot giant that represents the devil, he's showing that in the end, evil triumphs and dances on the graves of those that oppose him.

McCarthy teaches us that death offers an opportunity for fiction writers. Every book on the bookstore shelf concentrates on the *horizontal* narrative—what is happening to these characters, the description of this place, the A to Z plotline. But in good books, there is an additional *vertical* component, where the story taps into the common problems that have plagued all humans: What is the meaning of life? How can I love my neighbor? How do I avoid being evil?

In other words, any good story transcends its individual storyline and speaks to a broader truth about existence. So whenever you have a death in a book, you have a chance to add a vertical component to your book. What does it mean to live a good life? What does a good death look like?

One of my former professors was quite beloved. He was a pillar of the campus and a legend who'd taught for almost fifty years. Shortly after my time there, he got terminal cancer, and for one of his final addresses, he stood before the whole student body and said, "I've taught you how to live, and now I'm going to teach you how to die." And he did. He showed us how to die with dignity, with generosity, with grace, with forgiveness, and with a view firmly fixed on the afterlife. His horizontal storyline was just about getting cancer, and the year he underwent chemotherapy, and his slowly declining health. But his vertical storyline was about the meaning of death and how to live well.

When you show a death in your fiction, you are never only talking about that particular death. You are talking about universal Death. Don't shortchange the reader by only focusing on the plot elements of that death, and the way that it impacts the other characters. Stretch beyond to a philosophy of death and what the reader can learn from such a death. This is your chance to actually impart some wisdom, even if it's only a single line from one of your surviving characters.

For instance, in Flannery O'Connor's short story "A Good Man is Hard to Find," there is an outlaw called The Misfit who would be at home in anything written by Cormac McCarthy. In this story The Misfit murders a grandmother by putting three bullets in her chest. Afterward, he says, "She would of been a good woman if it had been somebody there to shoot her every minute of her life."

What vertical point is he making? That the pressure of impending death can have a tremendous effect on us. Perhaps he would agree with the Stoics that we should be pondering our own death as a way to live a better life. Or that we need a memento mori, an item that we can ponder that reminds us we will someday die. I just love that O'Connor chooses the villain to give us wisdom about how to live. "Out of the mouths of babes" . . . and brigands.

Let's talk about *how* to kill someone.

First, there is the invention part of the death process, which feels a little like a game of *Clue*. "In the Library, with the Wrench, killed by Miss Scarlet." This is the point when you look up that list online of 400+ ways to kill a character, available in some corner of the internet, and linger too long on the possibilities of autoerotic asphyxiation (sexy? Not really) and falling into a wood chipper (messy, but dynamic!). This is also the part where writers beg the FBI and NSA not to look too closely at their search histories. When the men in suits and sunglasses show up at your door and flash a badge, it's always difficult to explain that you were merely doing research on how long it takes to dissolve a person's bones in a tub of lye.

Now writers ask me all the time: How do I choose what character should die? If you're asking yourself this question, you should know it's the wrong question. You don't start with the idea that you're going to kill someone and play Russian roulette to find the victim. That's a vision of the author as a serial killer. A character death must rise organically from the personal storyline of that character, and from the overall storyline of the book. More often than not, writers don't plan these things out; they find themselves ambushed by the story. Let yourself be surprised to death.

As a reader of both published and unpublished manuscripts, the most frequent mistake I see in death scenes is rushing the process. A death is often the culmination of an entire storyline, the type of event that the reader has feared might happen for most of the book. And yet it's often given short thrift. A death happens and then we're onto the next stage without even as much as a space to breathe. This is a question of pacing, and you definitely have the right to linger on a moment like this.

Muriel Barbery, in *The Elegance of the Hedgehog*, kills one of the two main narrators of the book. The character's chasing someone along a street, and then boom—a van strikes her. It is one of the most surprising deaths I've read, not only because it wasn't foreshadowed, but because it's such a cerebral book. It's the type of book where you would never guess a character would die, which makes it the perfect book for a character to die.

What's curious is how Barbery handles this death. First, the actual moment comes like a slap: a two-word sentence announcing the event. "I die." You can't get any more direct than that. No literary artifice. No extravagant language. No complex sentence construction. Just the subject and the verb: stark and unyielding. And she bookends the chapter with almost the exact phrase, ending the chapter with "Peacefully, I die." Everything between those two points does two things.

First, it describes the sensations in the process of being flung from the impact: "It was only as I was falling, after a stunned moment of utter incomprehension, before the pain crushed me." And second, and more importantly, in the moment when the narrator is flying through the air, the author takes six pages—yes, six pages—to allow the narrator to address her friends. She's allowed time to say goodbye. To make a verbal will, of sorts. This helps the reader settle into the truth that she really is dying, and this isn't a trick. It also allows the reader the emotional space to process this huge and shocking event.

It's both a quick death and a slow death. The event itself is quick and shocks the reader. But what takes the length of two seconds in the reel of real life takes six pages in the book. The reading time elongates the moment and makes the reader dwell in this moment of tragedy.

Now why do so many writers struggle to slow down the pacing at a linchpin moment like this? It's because it's psychologically difficult to dwell on tragedy. So many writers instinctively shy away from conflict, even if they don't recognize it. And if you're saying to yourself—that's not me, I'm like a marine, I run toward the gunfire—that just means you haven't discovered the type of conflict you avoid. Perhaps you embrace physical conflict but struggle to linger on emotional conflict. Perhaps you like the conflict of war but struggle to take time for interpersonal conflict. Or perhaps there are just certain topics that are too personal for you to address in your writing. But every writer must overcome their natural instinct to avoid conflict and make the conscious decision to wallow, to linger, and to dwell in a tragic, conflict-heavy moment.

If you're failing to slow the pace at a critical moment like a death scene, you're failing to use the broad spectrum of tools available to a writer of words. In an era where storytellers and story consumers have flocked to cinema, preferring visual delights to the more difficult work of decoding language, remember that pacing is one of the main advantages a writer of words has over the screen. A movie has to progress at largely the same speed (barring an infrequent montage that symbolizes time passing). A movie can't speed up or slow down. While a book, on the other hand, can pass through ten years in a paragraph or take six pages for two seconds, all with the greatest of ease.

A second technique all writers should know is how to allude to a death. You don't always want death to stomp on your face. No, sometimes a gentle passing or a death off-screen is the appropriate move.

In Marilynne Robinson's *Gilead*, we also have a first-person narrator, John Ames. He knows he will die from a heart condition soon, and so the whole book works like an arrow, pointing toward that moment of death. Ames also worries about his wayward son Jack, who he believes will never come back to the fold, and Jack is the "you" he's writing to in the quote below. And this is how the book ends, with less of a bang and more of a whimper:

> I love this town. I think sometimes of going into the ground here as a last wild gesture of love—I too will smolder away the time until the great and general incandescence.
>
> I'll pray that you grow up a brave man in a brave country. I will pray you find a way to be useful.
>
> I'll pray, and then I'll sleep.

That final word, "sleep," is all we need to know that Ames died. It's a potent word, with subtext of death embedded in it. And if that wasn't enough, in the beginning of this quote he's thinking about being buried and the resurrection of the dead. This is such a quiet and gentle passing, with the actual death happening after the book's end, but we have enough clues to know for certain that he died.

A third technique you should know: how to temper your death. By temper I'm talking about an emotional reaction at odds with the emotion created by death. That means if you have a sad death, then try pairing it with an event that creates a positive emotion like happiness. This makes a death bittersweet.

Even if you haven't read it since childhood, you know *Charlotte's Web* by E. B. White. This is the end of the book, when Charlotte is dying:

"Good-bye," she whispered. Then she summoned all her strength and waved one of her front legs at him. She never moved again. Next day, as the Ferris wheel was being taken apart and the race horses were being loaded into vans and the entertainers were packing up their belongings and driving away in their trailers, Charlotte died. The Fair Grounds were soon deserted. The sheds and buildings were empty and forlorn. The infield was littered with bottles and trash. Nobody, of the hundreds of people that had visited the Fair, knew that a grey spider had played the most important part of all. No one was with her when she died.

This paragraph does wonderful work in creating mood and emotion. We have an abandoned location, pockmarked with trash. Words like "empty," "forlorn," and "nobody" do a lot of heavy lifting in darkening the mood. And then the final coffin slam of a sentence: "No one was with her when she died." The sheer loneliness, on top of the death itself, leaves you feeling bereft.

Yet the book doesn't end on that note. Just before she dies, she gave a special sack to Wilbur the pig to carry in his mouth and keep secure. This was her egg sack. So in the next and final chapter, all of her children hatch, ending the book with a happy nod toward her progeny living on. Yes, she died, but did so knowing her children would survive, and that creates a bittersweet emotion for the reader.

Remember that the happiness element could also simply be a line of dialogue. How often have you see a death scene in a film in which the character who is dying cracks a halfway humorous joke about their past, and the other character, who is crying, smiles through the tears? It seems like a joke would destroy the mood, but that momentary uplift only serves to deepen our sadness at the character dying. That's because a flatlining emotional reaction ends up deadening us to the feeling. We grow numb to our own sorrow. On the other hand, if in the middle of our sorrow we have a brief spike of happiness, we feel even more keenly the ensuing dip back down into sadness.

Now, almost all of the deaths we've looked at have been at the end of a book. That's because writers want readers to spend an entire book connecting with a character before they're cruelly snatched away. But how do you handle a death at the beginning of a book?

Alice Sebold answers that quite handily in her novel *The Lovely Bones*. Susie is fourteen years old and she is raped and murdered by a thirty-six-year-old on page 15 of a 328-page book. Even though we haven't had a lot of time to get to know Susie yet, we instinctively pity her because, obviously, she's a child being raped. She's innocent and wholesome, and we're already getting this story from her perspective, since she's in heaven narrating it after her death. Clearly, we know who deserves our sympathy. It's not our extensive knowledge of Susie that makes us empathize with her, it's her situation, a situation we all have a strong emotional reaction to.

But there is one other final element about this character death that's instructive. We are arriving at the end of the chapter, and we're sensing this will be the moment that Mr. Harvey kills Susie: "He leaned to the side and felt, over her head, across the ledge where his razor and shaving cream sat. He brought back a knife. Unsheathed, it smiled at me, curving up in a grin." Now, how would you move forward to write the death? Would you describe the stabbing? Would you describe the sensations? What level of detail would you offer?

The way Sebold handles this moment is masterful. She chooses to raise the stakes. By raising the stakes I mean make the moment even more poignant, even more awful, to ratchet up the emotional reaction from the reader. You wouldn't think that after depicting a child's rape and imminent murder, you would need to raise the stakes, but that's a frequent mistake by fledgling writers. You can *always* raise the stakes. No matter how awful or wonderful or absurdly funny a scene is, there is always a way to raise the stakes even more. And continuing to raise the stakes is what separates mediocre writers from great ones.

Here's how Sebold pulls it off: she has Mr. Harvey say, "Tell me you love me."

That's right. Just after raping Susie, and just before he slits her throat, he asks her to profess her love. And what's more, Susie says it, perhaps still hoping to save her life. Talk about twisting the knife. Just when you thought a death like this couldn't get more painful, Sebold finds a way to make you squirm.

And then Sebold gently alludes to the death itself—no gore, no specific details—with the briefly merciful line, "The end came anyway."

When I was eighteen years old, I hobnobbed around Egypt for a few weeks with three friends. We went to the Tomb of the Kings and snuck illicit photographs of the hieroglyphic walls, then visited the Pyramids of Giza, which we sprinted up until the guards climbed after us. We'd seen mummies hidden at the bottom of dry wells that weren't on any tourist route, exchanged fighting words with shopkeepers acting too friendly with our ladies, refused to pay camel owners after the camels bit my friend's leg, and gave a 100 percent tip to our day-use taxi driver after he took us to his house to eat a meal cooked by his wife. We were bedraggled, unshowered, and poor. I've never been so happy.

On our last night in Cairo, we finished dancing at a local wedding that we'd crashed, and then snatched catnaps on the lobby couches of a five-star hotel (eventually, they kicked us out). At three in the morning, we headed toward the other five-star hotel, hoping to crash on their couch for an hour before we went to the bus stop at 4:30 a.m. to catch a bus to Israel. To get to the other hotel, we had to cross a decently large street, empty because of the late hour, and dimly lit because, well, the infrastructure of Cairo was not exactly advanced. We scampered across, watching diligently for traffic because cars in Egypt do not obey any system of rules—not stoplights, or lanes, or pedestrian rights-of-way.

Just after we reached the other side, I heard a sound I've never forgotten. A screech of brakes and a thump, like someone punched a bag of wet flour. We turned to see a car stopped in the road, the headlights illuminating nothing. Behind them about forty feet was an unmoving body. They had been going fast, so fast that after they hit the woman it still took them a while to stop. Four men got out of the car and raced back to the figure lying still, so very still, in the street. They talked among themselves. Then the driver got back in and backed up the car. The woman on the ground was still not moving. Each of the men grabbed a limb and stuffed the woman in the backseat. How they fit a prone body plus all four of them in a tiny four-door, I don't know. The woman still wasn't moving. And then the car took off, going to what I hoped would be a hospital.

I've always wondered whether that woman lived or died. And even though I've seen my share of death, from the skeleton of my Aunt Janice as she withered away from colon cancer to the shock of watching the Twin Towers collapse from my twenty-first-floor apartment in the East Village, when I write about death I always think back to that woman in the street. I wonder whether the doctors were able to save her. I wonder how long it took them to contact the family. I wonder whether the four men should have called an ambulance instead, and whether moving her aggravated her injuries.

I'll never know the answers to those questions, but as I write fiction, I can finish the story. I can complete what is unknown. For some happy endings, perhaps I would let a character live. But some other endings, because I'm acquainted with the world and the way it bends toward darkness, I might have to let them die.

WRITING CHALLENGES:

1. Watch a soap opera or read a summary of one. Make a list of all the emotional cattle prods. Pick one to steal for your own fiction.
2. Write a few sentences describing how time passed over a decade for a particular character. Now write a hefty paragraph describing a one-second event in the life of that character.
3. Write a bittersweet paragraph. Include something as depressing as possible and pair it with the happiest thing you can think of. Contrast these two emotional polarities.
4. If you've written a death scene for a character, reread it and determine what techniques you're using. What in this chapter helps you to revise? Especially pay attention to pacing, allusion, and conflicting emotions. Also, look up three death scenes in books on your bookshelves and use them as inspiration and guidance for your death scene.
5. Think of a time when you personally experienced death. How can you mine that experience to write a character's death? What details can you steal and what emotions can you borrow and what dialogue can inspire you? Write a one-paragraph scene using that personal experience to show one of your characters dying, perhaps one you weren't planning on knocking off.

Further Reading: Google "How to Kill Your Characters Bookfox" to find more examples of character deaths.

12

THE LINCHPIN MOMENT

There's one final linchpin moment in the writer's life that we haven't talked about, but which is essential.

The moment you sit at your desk.

That action of bending your knees, lowering yourself into a chair, and facing a screen is the most essential and most heroic movement you can perform as a writer. It's a sacred moment, like entering a cathedral and kneeling. It says you are present, you are willing, and you will pay attention to what needs to be spoken through you today. No moment requires more humility—the blank page makes stooges of us all—and no action is more difficult to perform.

Writers know the terror of sitting down at the computer, but most haven't actually put it into words. It takes enormous reservoirs of courage to put words down in a line and then lift a bullhorn to your lips and shout to the world,

"This is worth your time! Devote your attention to what has sprung forth from my brain!"

To help us overcome this natural aversion, it might be good to recite a mantra as you sit down, a line that you repeat to yourself every moment before you begin to move your thoughts onto a page. I'll share one that I use, though feel free to create your own. This is a quote from Gandhi that I modified slightly for the writing life:

"Whatever I write today will be very insignificant, but it is very important that I do it."

It's counterintuitive, I know. You were probably hoping for something uplifting, a cheerleading kind of mantra:

I'm so smart and my words are a treat,
I'm full of ideas and cannot be beat!

But Gandhi was very wise. He wanted to show us that our life's work is a drop in the ocean of humanity. He actually said, "Whatever you *do* today will be very insignificant..." but the point holds for writers. Whatever we write will only make a ripple in history, no matter what level of fame you achieve.

The joy of this perspective is that it removes the burden. Some writers become paralyzed when they sit at the page because they feel like their life is at stake. Even veteran writers get paralyzed because they feel the weight of the books that have come before and the expectations of their readers. Fledgling writers are intimidated by the act of stepping into the ring with so many famous writers duking it out.

But by situating your writing in the context of every other writer now and throughout history, and in the activity of all other humans on earth, you get a better sense of

171

your tiny role to play. It lifts the weight from your writing. Create with joy, create with no expectations, create for the sheer pleasure of it—because there's no pressure!

But don't forget the second half of Gandhi's quote. In spite of your small role in the context of all human activity, it is *extremely* important that you write this book. How is that possible? How can your work be simultaneously insignificant and yet very important? First, it's very important because of what sitting down to the desk does for you as a person. Even if your book is never published, you are irrevocably changed by the act of writing it. You learn things about yourself.

For instance, it wasn't until years after I published my first book that I learned what it was truly about: all the characters struggling with physical maladies was not just a theme that happened to tie the book together, but was a way I was trying to process my own body falling apart, as I'd been diagnosed with reactive hypoglycemia, an inability to regulate my blood sugar, and was struggling to live with that debilitating condition. Writing that book with all the crazy maladies of my characters—synesthesia, Tourette's, epilepsy, Alzheimer's, mysterious poisonings, horrific sports injuries, and yes, one character suffering from reactive hypoglycemia—not only revealed to me how much my own condition weighed on me, it helped me process my health issues. This was not a theme I planned out. It was a theme that emerged naturally and that I discovered later as a window into my soul.

Writing your book will also give you a pride in yourself that can't be earned in a cheaper or easier way. Writing a book clads you with a next-level confidence that will assist you in all other areas of your life.

If I wrote a book, I can run a marathon.

If I wrote a book, I can lose this weight.

If I wrote a book, I can start dating again after my divorce.

If I wrote a book, I can find the stamina to raise my kids.

Your writing is also important because of the people who will read your book. Honestly, it doesn't matter the *number* of people who will read your book. Whether it's fifty or over a million, those were the lives you were destined to touch. Your book can bring healing, or laughter, or escapism, or freedom, or understanding. Your book can help someone feel less lonely, because they feel understood by you or they feel kinship with your character. You can help someone escape from a depressing life into a world of your creation and, for a few hours or more, set them free from the bondage of their life.

Gandhi's telling us the truth. Our writing is simultaneously insignificant and enormously important. And given that paradox, it's essential that today you perform the linchpin act of sitting in your chair and putting your fingers on the keyboard.

There will always be the common objections to sitting down at the desk. For instance, you might feel a crisis of confidence like that of the legendary poet Czeslaw Milosz. In his essay "Who Was I?" he writes that despite what he witnessed during World War II in Warsaw, he believed he didn't have anything to say. He worried that he was merely a poseur without any access to the truth, that no one should listen to him, and that he lacked the writing tools to handle huge themes like freedom and totalitarian governments.

He worried that being a writer was a distraction from what was more urgent, like fighting the Nazis and the horrors of the Holocaust, and that writing didn't matter. And yet he pushed through these fears and doubts and ended up winning the Nobel Prize in Literature. He writes: "One would like to astound the world, to save the world, but one can do neither. We are summoned to deeds that [matter] only to our village, our Catalonias, our Waleses, and our Slovenias."

You cannot save the world with your book, but you can reach your tribe: those who know you, those who live around you, those who care about your topic. If you have limited expectations—if you truly understand what Gandhi called your "insignificance"—then you are free to write what you are meant to write, and reach who you are meant to reach. You will be able to sit in the chair and write because you will have silenced that neurotic monkey on your shoulder, chattering naysayings into your ear.

Let me mention one other thing that hampers writers when they attempt the linchpin act of sitting in the chair. I once surveyed two thousand writers and asked them, "What is the main challenge you face as a writer?" More than 60 percent gave the same answer: "Time." It's so hard to find the time to write. It's hard to find time to spend in that chair. And yet finding the time is often finding the willpower, even when you're exhausted or your children need you or you hear the siren call of the dopamine-machines of social media or a new show has dropped on Netflix.

When you focus on carving out a huge block of time to sit in the chair, you're telling yourself multiple lies.

1. I can't write unless I get a huge chunk of time.
2. If my time is interrupted, it will ruin my concentration.

3. If I only had *more* time, I would be a better writer.
4. I'm not in control of my life; outside forces control me.

If you're struggling to find time to sit in the chair, then first of all understand that you have the most common problem known to writers. You are not a rare orchid; this is a problem that has been figured out by everyone who has ever written a book.

Second, your solution might be to artificially limit the time you have. That way you are not feeling like you're at the mercy of your life, but you are in control. I can't even emphasize how freeing this is, and how much your imagination can flourish when instead of feeling frustrated and time-trapped, you feel like the master of your domain.

Here's what I'm suggesting. Perhaps your previous goal was to have one hour for writing in the morning. Yet you wake up late, or go for a run instead, or the kid wakes up early and starts torturing the dog, or the spouse wakes up early and starts pawing at you for sexual favors. And so by the time that you've attended to that problem, half your time is gone and you throw up your hands and start making breakfast.

Instead of feeling that the world is pressing in on you and you have to press outward and fight for your hour to write, imagine that you have space throughout your day, so much luxurious space that you're choosing to use only part of it. Instead of being trapped in a tight bubble and pushing outward against it, imagine being in a wide-open field and drawing time toward you—selecting time at your leisure.

175

Here's the plan: instead of fighting to write for an hour, choose to write in fifteen-minute bursts. Suddenly, those fifteen minutes become the most important minutes of your life. It's astonishing what you can write in fifteen minutes. Perhaps you write so furiously that you accomplish more in those fifteen minutes than you previously did in an hour. And when you're done, and you still have a buffer of twenty minutes before you have another responsibility, you should not keep going, even if you have more ideas—you stop. You have to stop. And after you've stopped, you feel inspired and happy, rather than cramped and imprisoned. And so you look forward to the next fifteen-minute sprint. And have time to dream what you might write.

Lest you think I'm tooting hot air from an industrial-sized malarkey machine, let me tell you about my experience as a stay-at-home father of infant twins. I'd been teaching college courses in writing for over a decade when my wife and I finally succeeded at IVF and got pregnant with twin boys. It was a time of celebration and also of tough decisions: we decided my wife would keep working as a photography teacher, while I would quit being a professor and care for our duo of infants.

There's probably a joke to be made about how college freshmen and infants are not that different, but I will not make it because it's not true. It was a razor-sharp contrast and a tough transition, and not just because of sleep deprivation. In losing my work, I'd lost my identity. My masculinity was under siege every time someone asked, "So what do you do?" In fact, I used to put my twins in a double stroller and walk to the nearby community college just to be on a campus again, to see the kind of students I used to teach and long for the days of standing in front of a classroom. As a stay-at-home dad, I didn't know who I was or where I was going.

I decided to take this time to write. I had been writing before children, obviously, but always around the classes I was teaching and the papers I had to grade. Somehow I never got into a steady rhythm of writing. My days were fragmented, with each day a new schedule of commuting, each day new assignments to design.

Caring for twin newborns does not leave a great deal of space in the day (side note: I'm applying for Understatement of the Year Award). You can't leave them alone or else they'll eat a dust bunny or punch their brother in the face or reach down each other's diapers and spread the result on the wall. But I did find a rhythm. Before they were sleep trained, I couldn't wake up in the morning and put together a coherent phrase, because my brain had been broken by lack of sleep. But during naptimes, my brain mostly functioned and I designated that as my writing time.

The naptime was the most productive time of my writing life. I've never experienced anything like it. There's something about the ticking time bomb of a nap that accelerates your prose. At any moment there could be a stirring, a whimper, and any shot at finishing that paragraph will collapse. So I wrote with hurricane-force gusts, sweeping words onto the page. Every moment that I paused over the keyboard was a lost moment. I had the focus and intensity of a man on drugs. And there was an additional level of desperation because this novel was the only hope I had of a career. My teaching days were over, which left only writing as a goal.

All those wide-open meadows of time I had before children, when I was working as a professor? Somehow I didn't feel the urgency, and my output was meager. It was only when my time shrank that I became a writing machine. So don't tell yourself the lie that you don't have enough time. You can be more productive than ever before if you lose all your time. It's paradoxical, but less time can lead to more writing. All you have to do is fight to reclaim the small pockets of time you have left. (And if creating writing time is a perpetual struggle for you, I would recommend taking my online course "Master Your Writing Habits.")

I'd like to leave you with a story of someone who decided to sit at her desk, despite all the risks and opposition.

A fourteen-year-old girl from India reached out to me through Bookfox, asking the question that every aspiring author has: How do I become a writer? Now, I get a lot of emails from writers, especially young writers, who want me to mentor them, and sadly, I simply don't have the time. But a good friend of mine had recently challenged me to act like a philanthropist, to give generously of my time and money, and I had vowed to take action. So I wanted to help this girl.

What's more, her email was well written. So often when adults email me, the results are stiff, professional, and boring. This email, on the other hand, was entertaining and utterly raw. Even at her tender age, she was very smart. So we started emailing back and forth about writing, and a month later, on Christmas day, I offered to give her a gift of mentorship. She said it was the best Christmas present she'd ever received.

I'm going to call her Suzanne, because that's the pseudonym she originally contacted me under. Suzanne did not have an easy road to becoming a writer. If you're Indian, you might know the cultural pressure to shy away from the arts and focus on the sciences. Her parents hated that she wanted to become a writer. They said it was too risky because writers "don't earn money." In fact, when they discovered her writing, her parents sat her down and told her, directly, they were forbidding her to be a writer.

Besides those problems at home, her school didn't offer Literature as a subject. No teacher would talk to her about books or walk her through how to interpret a book. One teacher slapped her when she got low marks on a test, and another told her there was no reason to write unless she could earn money. And she had no way to buy books. Her family was exceptionally poor, too poor to invest money in purchasing a book. She couldn't even read online—her phone only gave her 100 Mb of internet a week, and she needed that for schoolwork and email. Sometimes she would borrow books from friends, but her parents got angry at her for this, because they believed it was taking charity from others. And even though I offered multiple times to mail her whatever book she wanted to read, she was always too proud to accept help.

Still, I encouraged Suzanne to keep a diary. And to write down any stories she dreamed up. And so she wrote in secret. And we kept emailing. She'd ask questions about writing, and I'd answer them. She sent me a piece that she wrote, and I gave her feedback. Honestly, her writing was fascinating—it had this raw emotional power stripped of any artifice. She wrote with a skill far beyond her years.

Then one day she emailed me, frantic, to tell me that her brother had discovered her diaries and given them to her parents, and her parents had thrown them all away. They made her promise to never write in a diary again. Years of her writing, her thoughts and secrets and stories, all lost to a trash can. And soon after that, even though she won a scholarship to a literature institute, they made her decline it.

But she couldn't stop writing. She wrote poetry and circulated it around her school anonymously. Soon her poems were being shared with every student, many copying them by hand and passing them on to other students, but nobody knew the author. And Suzanne had fun with her anonymity. She loved overhearing her classmates gossip about the identity of the mysterious writer, and loved watching people gasp and cry and laugh at her writing. Every Wednesday she'd write another poem and get her friend to start it circulating among the school, and by Friday, there were hundreds of copies of her poem, written in fifty different handwritings, making their rounds among her classmates.

But she confided to me that she worried that by continuing to write in secret, she was betraying her family's trust just to chase her dream. She said she felt a ton of guilt. And over multiple emails, she would close by begging me to tell her to give up writing. If I told her to give up writing, she promised she would give it up. Maybe if she gave it up, she thought, everything would be fine.

But I couldn't tell her to give it up. Even though I actually thought it might smooth over her family issues, I knew she had the hunger, and telling her to quit would kill her essential spark. And what's more, I've spent my entire life training people to write, and telling someone to quit contradicted every core principle of mine.

In the end, she was the one who decided to give up. Some bullies at her school discovered she was the author of the poems, and they stood up in class and exposed her, mocking some of her writing. They ended their mockery by actually ripping up the poems. She felt humiliated. She said she would never write again. She also said she'd never email me again. The bullies had defeated her in a way her parents and teachers never could.

I hoped this was just a momentary sadness, but I didn't hear from her for half a year, and worried she'd really given up. It was depressing to consider, but even when I reached out, she didn't return my emails. Some writers flame out, unfortunately, and there's nothing you can do. Finally, I got an email from her, and it contained the best and most hopeful news I could have imagined—she had finished a novel.

In that same email, she attacked the bullies: "But I don't give [the bullies] a damn. They don't own me. I own me and only I can stop me from becoming a writer."

She'd found the spark again. I emailed back congratulating her and suggested some ideas on how to develop as a writer. She took action:

- She started a writing group with her peers, where they all wrote pieces on a theme, such as "heartbreak." Her principal wanted to publish a book of them.
- She started a reading group, and they read fiction and talked for hours about it.
- She established a secret writing spot. It was in a forbidden place near her house, under a banyan tree. She often saw wild peacocks when she went there.

- Lastly, she had a long and hard conversation with her parents that made them finally understand her deep desire to become a writer. They didn't fully accept that desire, but it was a huge step.

Now, I don't know what hardships you face in your writing career. Maybe your obstacles are just as tough or even tougher than Suzanne's. But I think a story like this can teach us quite a bit. If, despite all the obstacles in her life, she can decide to keep putting words on the page, you can too.

Let's learn from her today. Let's stop at nothing to write the stories that mean the most to us.

Once, a mentor asked me, "Are you doing *everything* you can to achieve your goals as a writer?" And I had to admit that my desire to become a writer was outweighing my actions. I could do more. And I did. Just like Suzanne.

And now I pose the same question to you.

Are you doing everything you can to achieve your goals as a writer?

IF THIS BOOK INSPIRED YOU, DO THREE THINGS:

1. Review this book on Goodreads and Amazon.
2. Go to thejohnfox.com and join my newsletter.
3. Buy one of my writing courses or subscribe to all with Bookfox Academy.

ABOUT THE AUTHOR

J OHN MATTHEW FOX HELPS AUTHORS WRITE BETTER FICTION. He is the founder of Bookfox (thejohnfox.com), where he creates online courses for writers. His first book, "I Will Shout Your Name," was published by Press 53. After earning a creative writing MA from New York University and an MFA from the University of Southern California, he taught writing at the university level for a decade before devoting himself full time to Bookfox, which has been noted by *The Guardian*, *Los Angeles Times*, *Writer's Digest*, *Publisher's Weekly*, and *The Huffington Post*. His writing has also appeared in the *Chicago Tribune* and *Los Angeles Times*. Currently, he lives in Orange County, California.

Made in United States
Troutdale, OR
01/02/2024

16618102R00116